ENGLISH-SPANISH GUIDE FOR MEDICAL PERSONNEL

Compiled by

JOSEPH ARMENGOL, M.D.

JOSEPH   AMELAR

and

RICHARD D. AMELAR, M. D.

MEDICAL EXAMINATION PUBLISHING COMPANY, INC.
65-36 Fresh Meadow Lane
Flushing, New York 11365

1966

September 1966

TABLE OF CONTENTS

TABLE OF CONTENTS

NOTES ON PRONUNCIATION

SPANISH
Español
Ehs-pah-nyol

A - in Spanish pronounces as Ah

A - en español se pronuncia Ah
A - en ehs-pa-nyol seh pro-noon-syah Ah

E - Eh Note: There are no
I - Ee diphtongs in Spanish.
O - Oh Each vowel is pro-
U - Oo nounced separately,
as in:

¿Cuál? (Which?)
Día (Day)
Cien (100)

Nota: No hay diptongos en español.
Cada vocal es pronunciada
separadamente, como en:

¿Cuál? (Which?)
Día (Day)
Cien (100)

No-tah: No ah-ee deep-ton-gos en
ehs-pah-nyol. Cah-dah vo-
cal es pro-noon-syah-dah
seh-pah-rah-dah-mehn-teh,
co-mo ehn:

¿Cuál? (Which?)
Día (Day)
Cien (100)

U is silent when preceded by q and
followed by e or i, like:

¿Qué quiere? (What do you want?)

U - (Oo) es muda cuando la precede q
(Koo) y es seguida por e (eh) o i (ee)

U - ehs moo-dah kwan-do lah preh-seh-
deh q ee ehs seh-gee-dah por e (eh)
o i (ee), co-mo ehn:

¿Qué quiere? (What do you want?)
¿Ke kye-reh?

CE - pronounced as "thay," hard,

Hacer (to do)
ah-sehr

CE - pronunciada como "thay" en inglés
(seh-eh)

CI - pronounced as "thee," hard,

Nacido (born)
Nah-see-do

CI - pronunciada como "thee" en inglés
(seh-ee)

CH - pronounced as hard as in church
(Iglesia)
Muchacha (girl)
moo-chah-chah

CH - pronunciada como en church en
inglés

mucho (much)
moo-cho

D - At the beginning of words, same
as in English, but between two
vowels and at end of words,
pronounce soft, almost as "th":

dedo (finger)
usted (you)

D - Al principio de palabras, lo mismo
que en Inglés, pero entre dos vocales
y al fin de palabras, pronunciala
suave casi como "th" - (Deh)

D - Ahl preen-see-pee-o deh pah-lah-
bras, lo mees-mo ke ehn Een-glehs
peh-ro ehn-treh dos vo-ka-iehs ee
ahl feen deh pah-lah-brahs, pro-
noon-sya-lah sooa-veh kah-see ko-
mo "th"

dedo (finger) (deh-do)
usted (you) (oos-teh)

H - Is always silent:

hijo (son) ee-ho
hablar (to speak)
ah-blahr
ahora (now)
ah-ohrah

H (ah-cheh) es siempre sin sonido

J - Somewhat as hard "h" in
English:

jarro (pitcher)
ha-rro
José (Joseph)
Ho-seh

J - (ho-ta) Como más o menos "h" -
pero fuerte - en inglés:

Ko-mo mahs o meh-nos "h" peh-ro
foo-ehr-teh en Enh-glehs

LL - pronounced as "Y"

llamar (to call)
lya-mar
allí (there)
Ah-lly

LL - (el-lyay) como "Y"

(Ko-mo)

Ñ - as nee and sound next vowel as
usual:

año (year)
ah-nee-oh
niño (boy)
nee-nee-oh
niña (girl)
nee-nee-ah

Ñ - (eh-nee-eh) - como "nee" y pronuncie
la siguiente vocal como de costumbre:

ko-mo "nee" ee pro-noon-sy-eh lah see-
hee-ehn-teh vo-kal ko-mo deh kos-toom-
breh

QUE - pronounced "kay"

What do you want?

QUE - pronunciado "kay" en inglés.
(Ké)
pro-noon-sya-do "kay" ehn Een-glehs

¿Qué quiere usted?

¿Ké kye-reh oos-teth?

QUI - pronounced "Kee"

   quieto (quiet)
   Kee-eh-to

QUI - pronunciado "Kee"
(Kee)
pro-noon-syah-do kee

RR - Hard and rolling

   perro (dog)
   pehr-ro

RR - (doble ehr-reh)

   Fuerte y prolongando la "r" (ehr-reh_

   Foo-ehr-teh ee pro-lon-gan-do lah
   (ehr-reh)

S - Always hard at beginning and
end of words, and between
vowels

   (Never sound as Z (zee) but as
   S (eh-seh) in rose)

S - (eh-seh)
Siempre fuerte al principio y al final
de palabras, y entre vocales

   Syem-preh foo-ehr-teh ahl preen-
   see-pee-oh ee ahl fee-nal deh pah-
   lah-brahs, ee ehn-treh vo-kah-lehs.

   (Nunca pronuncie la "S" (eh-seh) como
   Z (seh-tah) sino como en rosa (rose)

Y - as a word in Spanish meaning
"and", is pronounced as "ee"
in English

Y - (ee-gree-eh-gah) como palabra en
español indica "and", es pronunciada
"ee" en inglés

   Ko-mo pah-lah-brah ehn ehs-pah-
   nyol een-dee-ka "and", ehs pro-
   noon-syah-dah "ee" ehn een-gles

- When a consonant, between
vowels, sounds like English Y:

   year (año)
     ah-nee-oh
   young (joven)
     ho-vehn

- Cuando es consonante, o entre vocales se pronuncia como "Y" en inglés:

   Kwan-do ehs con-so-nan-teh, o ehn-
   treh vo-ka-lehs she pro-noon-sya
   ko-mo "Y" ehn Een-gles

- At the end of a Spanish word
following a vowel like in:

   soy (I am)
     so-ee (verb ser)
   hay (there is)
     ah-ee
   estoy (I am)
     (verb estar)
     ehs-to-ee

- Al final de una palabra española después de una vocal como en:

   Ahl fee-nal deh oo-nah pah-lah-brah
   ehs-pah-nyo-lah dehs-pwes deh oo-
   nah vo-kal ko-mo ehn:

     soy (I am) (verb ser)
     so-ee
     hay (there is)

Rey (King)
R̲eh-ee

estoy (I am)
(verb est̲ar)
ehs-to̲-ee
Rey (Kiñg)
R̲eh-ee

is softly pronounced and the pre-
ceding vowel is somewhat prolonged.

es pronunci̲a̲da suaveme̲nte y la voc̲al que
le antec̲ede ̄se prol̲onga̅

ehs pro-noon-sy̲ah-dah soo-ah-veh-
men-teh ee lah vo-ka̅l ke leh ahn-teh-s̲eh-
deh̄ seh pro-l̲on-gah̄

SIMPLE RULES OF GRAMMAR

Verb To be - "Estar"
(indicating place, position, health, etc.)
(indicando lugar, posición, salud, etc.)
(een-dee-kan-do loo-gar, po-see-syon, sah-looth, etc.)

I am
    Yo estoy
      ee-oh ehs-to-ee

He is
    él está
      ehl ehs-tah

She is
    ella está (ella está en casa)
      eh-lya ehs-tah ehn ka-sah
      (She is at home)

We are
    Nosotros estamos
      no-so-tros ehs-tah-mos

You are (singular)
    Usted está (Usted está enferma)
      oos-teh ehs-tah ehn-fehr-mah
      (You are sick) (feminine)
      oos-teh ehs-tah ehn-fehr-mo
      (You are sick) (masculine)

You are (Plural)
    Ustedes están
      oos-teh-dehs ehs-tan

They are (masculine)
    ellos están
      eh-lyos ehs-tan

They are (feminine)
    ellas están (feminine)
      eh-lyas ehs-tan
      (ellas no están en casa)
      eh-lyas noh ehs-tan ehn kah-sah
      (They are not at home.)

I am not sick
    Yo no estoy enfermo (masculine)
      ee-o no ehs-to-ee ehn-fehr-mo

I am not sore
    Yo no estoy enfadado (masculine)
      ee-o no ehs-to-ee ehn-fah-dah-do
      enfadada (ehn-fah-dah-da (feminine)

ACCENTUATION

Words with regular accents are so shown. On other words where no accents are necessary, we show the accentuation by a small score under the vowel.

sangre (accent on a), blood - durante, during

SIMPLE WORDS AND EXPRESSIONS

PALABRAS Y EXPRESIONES SIMPLES
Pah-lah-brahs ee eks-preh-syo-nehs seem-plehs

ENGLISH

SPANISH
Ehs-pah-nyol

English	Spanish
I	Yo (ee-oh
He	él (ehl)
She	élla (eh-lya)
You (singular)	usted (oos-teth
You (plural)	ustedes (oos-teh-dehs)
They (masculine)	ellos (eh-lyos)
They (feminine)	ellas (eh-lyas)

VERB "TO BE"

VERBO "SER" (Sehr)

English	Spanish
I am	soy (so-ee)
He is	él es (ehl ehs)
She is	ella es (eh-lya ehs)
We are	nosotros somos (no-so-tros soh-mohs)
You are (singular)	usted es (oos-teh ehs) (singular)
You are (plural)	ustedes son (oos-teh-dehs son)
They are (masculine)	ellos son (eh-lyos son) (masculine)
They are (feminine)	ellas son (eh-lyas son) (feminine)

SOME USEFUL VOCABULARY

This (masculine) este
        ehs-teh

este hombre - this man
ehs-teh om-breh

This (feminine) esta
        ehs-tah

esta señora - this lady
ehs-tah seh-nyo-ra

This - as pron. demonstrative
    neutral - esto

esto (ehs-to) - this

    Esto no es mío

This is not mine
ehs-to no ehs mee-oh

    Esto es suyo

This is yours
ehs-to ehs soo-ee-oh

What is this?

¿Qué es esto?
Ke ehs ehs-to

This is

Esto es (ehs-to ehs)

It is

Lo es (lo ehs)

Yes, Sir

Si, señor
see-seh-nyor

Yes, Madam

Si, señora
see seh-nyo-rah

No, Sir

No, señor
Noh, seh-nyor

Si, señorita

Yes Miss
see seh-nyo-ree-tah

Who is it?

¿Quién es?
¿Kyen ehs?

And "Y" (ee) but before "i" and
   "hi", use "é" (eh)

       father and son

padre é hijo
pah-dreh eh ee-ho

Or "O" but before "O" and "HO" use
   "U" (oo)

       ear or eye

oreja u ojo
oh-reh-ha oo oh-ho

       book or leaf

libro u hoja
lee-bro oo oh-ha

He and I

El y yo
ehl ee ee-o

She and I

Ella y yo
eh-lya ee ee-o

The art. masculine El

El libro - The book
ehl lee-bro

The art. feminine La

La mesa - The table
lah meh-sah

The art. mas. plural

Los libros - The books
los lee-bros

The art. fem. plural

Las mesas - The tables
lahs meh-sahs

A - un (mas.) (oon)

Un hombre - A man
oon om-breh

A - una (fem.) (oo-nah)

Una mujer - A women
oo-nah moo-hehr

Some - (mas.)

Unos hombres - Some men
oo-nos om-bres

Some - (fem.)

Unas mujeres - Some women
oo-nahs moo-he-rehs

Where?

¿Dónde?
¿don-deh?

From where?

¿De dónde?
¿deh don-deh?

Where is?

¿Dónde está?
¿don-deh ehs-tah?

Where are you going?

¿A dónde va usted?
¿ah don-deh vah oos-teth?

How?

¿Cómo?
¿ko-mo?

How much?

¿Cuánto?
¿Kwan-to?

When?

¿Cuándo?
¿Kwan-do?

Enough

Bastante
bahs-tahn-teh

Some Useful Vocabulary

Now
Ahora
ah-oh-rah

After
Después
dehs-poo-ehs

Again
Otra vez
o-trah vehs

ENGLISH	SPANISH
Verb - "To Have"	Verbo - Tener (teh-nehr)
I have	(Yo) tengo (ee-o) tehn-go
He has	El tiene ehl tye-neh
She has	Ella tiene eh-lya tye-neh
You (singular)	Usted tiene oos-teth tye-neh
You (plural)	Ustedes tienen oos-teh-dehs tye-nehn
We have (masculine)	Nosotros tenemos no-so-tros teh-neh-mos
We have (feminine)	Nosotras tenemos no-so-trahs teh-neh-mos
They have (masculine)	Ellos tienen eh-lyos tye-nehn
They have (feminine)	Ellas tienen eh-lyas tye-nehn
I have not	Yo no tengo ee-o no tehn-go
Do you have?	¿Tiene usted? tye-neh oos-teth
Does he have?	¿Tiene él? tye-neh ehl
What do you have? What ails you?	¿Qué tiene usted? or ¿Qué le pasa? ke tye-neh oos-teth? or ¿ke leh pah-sah?

What is wrong with her?	¿Qué tiene ella? or ¿Qué le pasa a ella?
What ails her?	ke tye-neh eh-lya? or ¿ke leh pah-sah ah eh-lya?

Verb - "To Wish" or "To Want"	Verbo - Querer (keh-rehr)
I wish or I want	Yo quiero
	ee-o kee-eh-ro
He wishes	El quiere
	ehl kee-eh-reh
She wishes	Ella quiere
	eh-lya kee-eh-reh
We wish (masculine)	Nosotros queremos
	no-so-tros keh-reh-mos
We wish (feminine)	Nosotras queremos
	no-so-trahs keh-reh-mos
You wish (singular)	Usted quiere
	oos-teth kee-eh-reh
You wish (plural)	Ustedes quieren
	oos-teth-dehs kee-eh-rehn
They wish (masculine)	Ellos quieren
	eh-lyos kee-eh-rehn
They wish (feminine)	Ellas quieren
	eh-lyas kee-eh-rehn
Do you wish something?	¿Quiere usted algo?
	¿kye-reh oos-teth ahl-go?
What do you want?	¿Qué quiere usted?
	ke kye-reh oos-teth
I do not want anything	No quiero nada
	no kye-ro nah-dah
What does she want?	¿Qué quiere ella?
	¿ke kye-reh eh-lya?
She does not want anything	Ella no quiere nada
	eh-lya no kye-reh nah-dah
Nothing	Nada
	nah-dah
Good morning, Sir	Buenos días, señor
	boo-eh-nos dyas, seh-nyor

Good afternoon, Miss	Buenas tardes, señorita Boo-eh-nahs tahr-dehs seh-nyo-ree-tah
Good evening, Mrs.	Buenas noches, señora Boo-eh-nahs no-chehs, seh-nyo-rah
Good night, Mrs.	Buenas noches, señora Boo-eh-nahs no-chehs, seh-nyo-rah
So long	Hasta la vista ahs-tah lah vees-tah
Good bye	Adios ah-dee-os
How are you?	¿Cómo está usted? ko-mo ehs-tah oos-teh
Very well, thank you	Muy bien, gracias moo-ee byen grah-see-ahs
I am very glad	Me alegro mucho meh ah-leh-gro moo-cho
Here	Aquí ah-kee
There	Allí ah-lyee
There	Allá - showing further distance) ah-lya
My book	Mi libro mee lee-bro
Your house	Su casa soo kah-sah
His, her table	Su mesa soo meh-sah
Already	Ya ee-ah
Did you eat already?	¿Ya comió usted ? ¿ee-ah co-mee-o oos-teth
What did you eat?	¿Qué comió usted? ¿ke co-mee-o oos-teth?
I have eaten	Yo he comido ee-o eh co-mee-do

I have not eaten	Yo no he comido ee-o no eh co-mee-do
To eat	Comer co-mehr
To drink	Beber beh-behr
Verb "To Have" (auxiliary)	Verbo "Haber" (ah-behr)
I have received	Yo he recibido ee-o eh reh-see-bee-do
He has eaten	El ha comido ehl ah co-mee-do
She has given	Ella ha dado eh-lya ah dah-do
We have had	Nosotros hemos tenido no-so-tros eh-mos teh-nee-do
You have (singular)	Usted ha oos-teth ah
You have (plural)	Ustedes han oos-teh-dehs ahn
They have (masculine)	Ellos han eh-lyos ahn
They have (feminine) come	Ellas han venido eh-lyas ahn veh-nee-do
What have they given?	¿Qué han dado ellos? ¿ke ahn dah-do eh-lyos?
What has she eaten?	¿Qué ha comido ella? ¿ke ah co-mee-do eh-lya?
What has happen?	¿Qué ha pasado? ¿ke ah pah-sah-do?
I do not know	No lo sé (meaning I do not know it) no loh seh
What do you know?	¿Qué sabe usted? ¿ke sah-beh oos-teth?
I do not know anything	No sé nada no seh nah-dah

Nothing	Nada nah-dah
Which is?	¿Cuál es? Kwal ehs
Cold water	Agua fría ah-goo-ah free-ah
Hot water	Agua caliente ah-goo-ah kah-lyen-teh
Lukewarm water	Agua tibia ah-goo-ah tee-bee-ah
A glas (of)	Un vaso (de) oon vah-so (deh)
Thank you	Muchas gracias moo-chas grah-syas
Your are welcome	No hay de que no ah-ee deh-keh
Tablespoon	Cuchara koo-cha-rah
Tablespoonful	Cucharada koo-cha-rah-dah
Teaspoon	Cucharita koo-cha-ree-tah
Teaspooful	Cucharadita koo-cha-rah-dee-tah
A great deal	Mucho moo-cho
Very much	Muchísimo moo-chee-see-mo
A little	Un poco oon po-ko
A very little	Un poquito oon po-kee-to
What is your name?	¿Cómo se llama usted? ¿co-mo seh lya-mah oos-teth?
How old are you?	¿Qué edad tiene usted? ¿ke eh-dahd tye-neh oos-teth?

Where were you born?	¿Dónde nació usted? ¿don-deh nah-syo oos-teth?
Where do you live?	¿Dónde vive usted? ¿don-deh vee-veh oos-teth?
What is your religion?	¿Cuál es su religión? ¿kwal ehs soo reh-lee-ghee-on?
Catholic	Católico ka-to-lee-co
Protestant	Protestante pro-tehs-tan-teh
Jewish	Hebreo (or judío) eh-breh-oh (o hoo-dyo)
WEEK DAYS	DIAS DE LA SEMANA dyas deh lah seh-mah-nah
Sunday	domingo do-meen-go
Monday	lunes loo-nehs
Tuesday	martes mahr-tehs
Wednesday	miércoles mee-ehr-co-lehs
Thursday	jueves hoo-eh-vehs
Friday	viernes vee-ehr-nehs
Saturday	sábado sah-bah-do
This morning	Esta mañana ehs-tah mah-nya-nah
This afternoon	Esta tarde ehs-tah tahr-deh
Tonight	Esta noche ehs-tah no-cheh
Tomorrow	Mañana mah-nya-nah

After tomorrow	Pasado mañana pah-sah-do mah-nya-nah
Tomorrow morning	Mañana por la mañana mah-nya-nah por lah mah-nya-nah
Yesterday	Ayer ah-yehr
Day before yesterday	Anteayer ahn-teh-ah-yehr
MONTH(S)	MES (MESES - plural)
January	Enero eh-neh-ro
February	Febrero feh-breh-ro
March	Marzo mahr-so
April	Abril ah-breel
May	Mayo mah-yo
June	Junio hoo-nyo
July	Julio hoo-lyo
August	Agosto ah-gos-to
September	Septiembre sehp-tyem-breh
October	Octubre ock-too-breh
November	Noviembre no-vyem-breh
December	Diciembre dee-syem-breh
Year(s)	Año (Años - plural) ah-nyo (ah-nyos)

This year   Este año
                                   ehs-teh ah-nyo

Next year   El año próximo
                                   ehl ah-nyo prok-see-mo

Last year   El año pasado
                                   ehl ah-nyo pah-sah-do

What year?   ¿Qué año?
                                   ke-ah-nyo

How many years?   ¿Cuántos años?
                                   kwan-tos ah-nyos

One year ago   Hace un año
                                   ah-seh oon ah-nyo

Two years ago   Hace dos años
                                   ah-seh dos ah-nyos

Since when?   ¿Desde cuándo?
                                   dehs-deh kwan-do

Since this morning   Desde esta mañana
                                   dehs-de ehs-tah mah-nya-nah

It is alright   Está bien
                                   ehs-tah byen

NUMBERS   NUMEROS
                                   noo-meh-ros

1 - uno   oo-no
2 - dos   dos
3 - tres   trehs
4 - cuatro   kwa-tro
5 - cinco   syn-ko
6 - seis   seh-ees
7 - siete   see-eh-teh
8 - ocho   oh-cho
9 - nueve   noo-eh-veh
10 - diez   dee-ehs
11 - once   on-seh
12 - doce   do-seh
13 - trece   treh-seh
14 - catorce   ka-tor-seh
15 - quince   keen-seh
16 - diez y seis   dee-ehs ee seh-ees
17 - diez y siete   dee-ehs ee see-eh-teh
18 - diez y ocho   dee-ehs ee oh-cho
19 - diez y nueve   dee-ehs ee noo-eh-veh
20 - veinte   veh-een-teh

21 - veinte y uno (or veintiún)   veh-een-teh ee oo-no o veh-een-tee-oon
22 - veinte y dos (or veintidos)   veh-een-teh ee dos o veh-een-tee-dos

30 - treinta   treh-een-tah
31 - treinta y uno   treh-een-tah ee oo-no

40 - cuarenta   kwa-rehn-tah
50 - cincuenta   syn-kwen-tah
60 - sesenta   seh-sen-tah
70 - setenta   seh-tehn-tah
80 - ochenta   oh-chehn-tah
90 - noventa   no-vehn-tah

100 - cien   syen
200 - dos cientos   dos syen-tos

First   primero
                                         pree-meh-ro

The first   el primero (masculine)
                                         ehl pree-meh-ro

The first   la primera (feminine)
                                         lah pree-meh-rah

Second   segundo
                                         seh-goon-do

Third   tercero
                                         tehr-seh-ro

Fourth   cuarto
                                         kwar-to

Fifth   quinto
                                         kyn-to

What day?   ¿Qué día?
                                         ke dee-ah

What month?   ¿Qué mes?
                                         ke mehs

What year?   ¿Qué año?
                                         ke ah-nyo

The first of January   El día primero de enero
                                         ehl dee-ah pree-meh-ro deh eh-neh-ro

Who is first (masculine)?   ¿Quién es el primero?
                                         kyen ehs ehl pree-meh-ro

Who is first (feminine)?	¿Quién es la primera? kyen ehs lah pree-meh-ra
First time	Primera vez pree-meh-rah vehs
Last time	Ultima vez ool-tee-mah vehs
Each time	Cada vez Ka-dah vehs
Some other time	Alguna otra vez Ahl-goo-nah oh-trah vehs

INTERVIEWING THE PATIENT
Entrevistando al Paciente
Ehn-treh-vees-tah̄n-do ahl pah̄-see-ehn-teh

ADMITTING OFFICE

OFICINA DE ADMISIONES
O-fee-see-nah deh ad-mee-syo-nes

Who is the patient?

¿Quién es el paciente?
kyen ehs ehl pah-syen-teh

What is your name?

¿Cómo se llama?
ko-mo seh lya̅-mah

Your age?

¿Qué edad tiene?
ke eh-dath tye̅-neh

Date of birth?

¿Fecha de nacimiento?
fe̅-cha deh nah-see̅-myen-toh

Where were you born?

¿Dónde nació?
don-deh na-syo

How long have you been in U.S.A.?

¿Cuánto tiempo tiene en los Estados
Unidos de América?
kwan̄-to tyem-po tye-neh ehn los
Ehs̄-tah-dos Oo-nee̅-thos deh
Ah-meh̄-ree-ka

How long have you lived in N.Y.C.?

¿Cuánto tiempo ha vivido en Nueva
York?
kwan̄-to tyem-po ah vee-veeh-tho
ehn̄ Noo-eh-vah York

Your address?

¿Su domicilio?
soo do-mee̅-see̅-lyo

Private home?

¿Casa privada?
kah-sah pree-vah-thah

Apartment?   What number?

¿Apartamento? ¿Qué número?
ah-par-tah̄-mehn-toh ke noo-meh-roh

Telephone?   Number?

¿Teléfono?   ¿Número?
teh-leh-foh-noh noo-meh-ro

Postal zone?

¿Zona postal?
soh-nah pohs-tahl

Are you single?

¿Es usted soltero?
ehs oos-teh sohl-teh-ro
ehs oos-teh sohl-teh̄-rah (feminine)

Are you married?

¿Es usted casado?
ehs oos-teh kah-sah-tho
ehs oos-teh kah-sah-tha (feminine)

Widower?

¿Viudo?
vyu-tho
vyu-tha (feminine)

Divorced?

¿Divorciado?
dee-vohr-see-ah-tho
dee-vohr-see-ah-tha (feminine)

Separated?

¿Separado?
seh-pah-rah-tho

What kind of work do you do?

¿Qué clase de trabajo hace usted?
ke klah-seh deh trah-bah-ho a-seh oos-teth

What is your religion?

¿Cuál es su religión?
kwal ehs soo re-lee-hyon

The name of the company or
place where you work?

¿El nombre de la compañía?   ¿Lugar dónde
trabaja?
ehl nom-breh deh lah com-pah-nya
loo-gahr don-deh trah-bah-ha

The address of your employment?

¿La dirección donde trabaja?
lah dee-rek-syon don-deh trah-bah-ha

What is your social security
number?

¿Cuál es su número de seguro social?
Kwal ehs soo noo-meh-roh dehl seh-goo-roh
soh-syal

Is this a compensation case?

¿Es este caso de compensación?
ehs es-teh kah-so deh kom-pen-sah-syon

Have you any Insurance?

¿Tiene usted algún seguro?
tye-neh oos-teth ahl-goon seh-goo-roh

Blue Shield?

¿Escudo Azul?
ehs-koo-tho ah-sool

Blue Cross?

¿Cruz Azul?
Kroos Ah-sool

Any other?

¿Algún otro seguro?
al-goon-oh-troh seh-goo-ro

What are the numbers of your
policies?

¿Cuáles son los números de sus pólizas?
Kwa-les son los noo-me-ros deh soos po-
lee-sas

Who is going to pay the bills?

¿Quién va a pagar los gastos?
kee-ehn vah ah pah-gar los gas-tos

Is this a liability case?

¿Es este caso de asunto legal o de abogados?
ehs ehs-teh kah-so deh ah-soon-toh leh-gal oh deh ah-boh-gah-thos

What is your wife's name?

¿Cuál es el nombre de su esposa?
Kwal- ehs ehl nom-breh deh soo ehs-poh-sah

What is your husband's name?

¿Cuál es el nombre de su esposo?
Kwal ehs ehl nom-breh deh soo ehs-poh-soh

In case of emergency who is to be notified?

¿En caso de emergencia a quién se notifica?
Ehn cah-soh deh eh-mehr-hen-see-ah ah kee-ehn seh noh-tee-fee-kah

Who is this person?

¿Quién es esta persona?
Kyen ehs ehs-tah per-soh-nah

A relative?

¿Pariente?
pah-ryen-teh

What relation?

¿Qué relación?
ke reh-lah-syon

A friend?

¿Amigo? (male)
ah-mee-goh

¿Amiga? (female)
ah-mee-gah

A neighbor?

¿Vecino? (male)
veh-see-noh

¿Vecina? (female)
veh-see-nah

What is this person's address and telephone?

¿Cuál es la dirección y teléfono de esta persona?
Kwal ehs lah dee-rek-syon ee teh-leh-foh-no deh ehs-tah per-soh-nah

The full name of your:

¿Nombre completo de su:
nom-breh kohm-pleh-toh deh soo:

Father

¿Padre?
pah-threh

Mother (maiden name)?

¿Madre? (nombre de soltera)
mah-threh (nom-breh deh sol-teh-rah

Are your parents dead or alive?

¿Sus padres están vivos o muertos?
soos pah-thres ehs-tahn vee-vohs o
moo-ehr-tos

Where were your parents born?

¿Dónde nacieron sus padres?
don-deh nah-syeh-ron soos pah-thres

What is your weekly salary?

¿Cuánto gana por semana?
Kwan-toh gah-nah por seh-mah-nah

Do you own your home?

¿Es usted propietario de su casa?
Ehs oos-teth pro-pye-tah-ryo deh soo
cah-sah

Do you receive money from:

the government?

¿Recibe dinero de el gobierno?
re-see-beh dee-neh-roh deh ehl goh-
byer-no

insurances?

¿seguros?
seh-goo-ros

compensation?

¿compensación?
kom-pen-sah-syon

any investment?

¿de algún otro negocio?
deh al-goon o-tro ne-go-syo

How much is the mortgage?

¿Cuánto es la hipoteca?
Kwan-to ehs lah ee-poh-teh-kah

How much is your rent?

¿Cuánto es la renta?
Kwan-to ehs lah ren-tah

Have you bank accounts and savings?

¿Tiene usted cuenta corriente con algún
banco o cuenta de ahorros?
tye-neh oos-teth kwen-tah ko-rryen-teh
kohn al-goon ban-koh o kwen-tah theh
ah-oh-rrohs

Do you get home relief?

¿Recibe ayuda del departamento de
ayuda social?
Reh-see-veh ah-yoo-tha dehl theh-part-
tah-mehn-toh deh ah-yoo-tha soh-see-ahl

Who supports you?

¿Quién lo mantiene?
Kyen lo mahn-tye-neh
¿Quién la mantiene? (feminine)
Kyen lah mahn-tye-neh

Name the person supporting you?

¿Nombre la persona que lo (la - fem.)
ayuda?
Nom-bre deh lah per-soh-nah ke lo (la)
ah-yoo-tha

Is this person related to you?	¿Es esta persona pariente suyo (suya - fem.)? ¿o un amigo (amiga- fem.)?
or a friend?	ehs ehs-tah per-soh-nah pah-ree-ehn-teh soo-yoh (soo-yah - feminine) oh oon ah-mee-go (ah-mee-gah - feminine)
Give the address, the telephone number and occupation of your relative (or friend)?	¿Deme la dirección, número de teléfono y ocupación de su pariente (o amigo - o amiga - fem.) deh-meh lah dee-rek-syon, noo-meh-ro dehl teh-leh-foh-no ee o-koo-pah-syon
Have you been in this hospital before? How many times?	¿Ha estado en este hospital antes? ¿Cuántas veces? ah ehs-tah-tho ehn ehs-teh ohs-pee-tal ahn-tehs kwan-tahs veh-sehs
On what dates were you hospitalized?	¿En qué fechas estuvo hospitalizado? Ehn ke feh-chas ehs-too-voh os-pee-tah-lee-zah-tho
Have you been in other hospital? Which one?	¿Ha estado en otro hospital? ¿En cuál? ah ehs-that-tho ehn o-tro os-pee-tahl Ehn kwal
Have you been under doctor's care?	¿Ha estado bajo cuidado de doctor? ah ehs-tha-tho bah-ho kwee-tha-tho deh dok-tor
What is his name, address, and telephone number?	¿Cuál es el nombre del doctor, la dirección y el teléfone? Kwal ehs ehl nom-bre dehl dok-tor, lah dee-rek-syon ee ehl teh-leh-foh-no
What is your complaint?	¿De qué se queja usted? deh ke seh ke-ha oos-teth
When did you receive the injuries?	¿Cuándo recibió las heridas? kwan-do re-see-byo las eh-ree-thas
Go to the Emergency Room	Vaya a la sala de emergencia vah-yah ah lah sah-lah deh e-mer-hen-see-ah
Sign here	Firme aquí Feer-meh a-kee

TAKING THE MEDICAL HISTORY

What is your trouble?	¿Cuál es su mal? kwal ehs soo mahl
Pains? Where?	¿Dolores? ¿Dónde? do-lo-res don-de
Weakness?	¿Debilidad? de-bee-lee-thad
Dizziness?	¿Mareo? ma-re-o
Nauseà or vomiting?	¿Nausea o vómito? Naoo-se-a oh voh-mee-toh
Belching and flatulence?	¿Erutando y pasando gases? e-roo-tan-do ee pa-san-do ga-ses
Heartburn?	¿Ardor de estomago? ar-dor de es-to-ma-go
Constipated?	¿Estreñido? ¿Estreñida? (fem.) es-tre-nee-tho es-tre-nee-tha
Color of your stools?	¿Color de su escremento? ko-lor de soo es-cre-men-to
Any blood or mucus?	¿Con sangre o moco? kon san-gre o mo-ko
Did you have intestinal parasites?	¿Ha tenido parásitos intestinales? ah te-nee-tho pa-ra-see-tos een-tes-tee-na-les
Have you lost weight?	¿Ha perdido peso? ah per-dee-do pe-so
Are you feverish?	¿Se siente con fiebre? se syen-te kon fye-bre
Have you been jaundiced?	¿Ha tenido ictericia? ah te-nee-do eek-te-ree-see-a
Have you malaise?	¿Se siente con mal estar general? se syen-te con mal-es-tar ge-ne-ral
Have you any urinary trouble?	¿Tiene algún trastorno con la orina? tye-ne al-goon tras-tor-no con la o-ree-nah

Are you nervous?	¿Es usted nervioso (a) (fem.)? es oos-teh ner-vyo-so (a)
Can you sleep well? How many hours?	¿Puede dormir bien? ¿Cuántas horas? pwe-de dor-meer byen kwan-tas o-ras
Do you smoke? How much?	¿Fuma? ¿Cuánto? foo-ma kwan-to
Do you drink alcoholic beverages?	¿Bebe bebidas alcohólicas? be-be be-bee-das al-ko-o-lee-kas
Do you drink to excess, in moderation or only occasionally?	¿Bebe en exceso, en moderación, o solamente en ocasiones? be-be en ek-se-so, en mo-de-ra-syon o en o-ca-syo-nes
Do you drink coffee, or tea, or both?	¿Bebe café o té o ambos? be-be ca-fe o te o am-bos
Do you take narcotic or sedatives or both?	¿Toma narcóticos, o sedativos, o ambos? to-ma nar-ko-tee-kos, o se-da-tee-vos, o am-bos
Do you have menstrual disturbances?	¿Tiene trastornos con la menstruación? tye-ne tras-tor-nos con la mens-troo-a-syon
When did you have the last period?	¿Cuándo tuvo el último periodo? kwan-do too-bo el ool-tee-mo pe-ryo-do
Did you have children?	¿Cuántas criaturas ha tenido? kwan-tas crya-too-ras ah te-nee-do
What diseases have you had in your life time?	¿Qué enfermedades ha tenido durante su vida? ke en-fer-me-da-des ah te-nee-do doo-ran-te soo vee-da
What diseases have been in your family and ancestors?	¿Qué enfermedades han habido en su familia y predecesores? ke en-fer-me-da-des an ah-bee-do en su fa-mee-lya ee pre-de-se-so-res
Tuberculosis?	¿Tuberculosis? too-ber-koo-lo-sees
Syphilis?	¿Sifilís? see-fee-lees
Cancer?	¿Cancer? kan-ser

Arterial hypertension?	¿ Presión alta de sangre? pre-syon al-ta de san-gre
Renal diseases?	¿ Enfermedades de los riñones? en-fer-me-da-des de los ree-nee-o-nes
Diabetes mellitus?	¿ Diabetes dulce? dya-be-tes dool-se
Mental diseases?	¿ Casos mentales? ka-sos men-ta-les
Arteriosclerosis?	¿ Arterio-esclerosis? ar-te-ryo-es-cle-ro-sys
Pernicious anemia?	¿ Anemia perniciosa? a-ne-mya per-nee-syo-sa
Bleeding tendencies?	¿ Tendencias a sangrar? ten-den-syas a san-grar
Heart diseases?	¿ Enfermedades del corazón? en-fer-me-da-des del co-ra-son
Any other disease?	¿ Alguna otra enfermedad? al-goo-na o-tra en-fer-me-thad

PARTS OF THE BODY	PARTES DEL CUERPO Par-tes del kwer-po
Have you had any pains in the ears?	¿Ha tenido dolores en las orejas? ah te-nee-tho do-lo-res en las o-reh-has
The head	La cabeza la ka-beh-sah
eyes	Los ojos los o-hos
nose	La nariz la nah-reeth
mouth	La boca la bo-ka
ears	Las orejas las orejas (la oreja - singular) las o-reh-has (la o-reh-ha)
teeth	Los dientes los dyen-tes (diente - singular)
gums	Las encías las en-see-as
tongue	La lengua la len-goo-ah
neck	El cuello el kwe-lyo
chest	El pecho el peh-cho
stomach	El estómago el es-to-ma-go
abdomen or belly	Abdomen o vientre ab-do-men o vyen-tre
hands	Las manos (la mano - singular) las ma-nos (la ma-no)
arms	Los brazos (el brazo - singular) los brah-sos (el bra-so)
feet	Las piernas (la pierna - singular) las pyer-nas (la pyer-na)

legs

Las piernas (la pierna - singular)
las pyer-nas (la pyer-na)

body

El cuerpo
el kwer-po

back

la espalda
la ehs-pal-da

joints

Las articulaciones (la articulación - sing.)
las ar-tee-coo-lah-syo-nes

buttoks

Las nalgas (la nalga - singular)
las nal-gas

MUSCULO-SKELETAL SYSTEM
AND SKIN

SISTEMA MUSCULO-ESQUELETAL
Y PIEL
Sees-te-ma moos-koo-lo-es-ke-le-tal
ee pyel

Have you had any loss of weight?

¿Ha tenido usted alguna pérdida de peso?
ah te-nee-tho oos-teth al-goo-na per-dee-
tha de pe-so

Have you had weakness?

¿Ha tenido usted debilidad?
ah te-nee-tho oos-teth de-bee-lee-thad

Have you had any fever?

¿Ha tenido usted fiebre?
ah te-nee-tho oos-teth fye-bre

Have you had sweating?

¿Ha tenido usted sudores?
ah te-nee-tho oos-teth soo-do-res

Have you had any chills?

¿Ha tenido usted escalofríos?
ah te-nee-tho oos-teth es-ka-lo-fryos

Do you get tired easily?

¿Se cansa usted fácilmente?
se kan-sa oos-teth fa-seel-men-te

Have you had any jaundice?

¿Ha sufrido usted de ictericia?
ah soo-free-tho oos-teth de eek-te-ree-
sya

Yellowish skin color

Color amarillo de la piel
ko-lor a-ma-ree-lyo de la pyel

Have you had any purpura (blood
spots) on the skin?

¿Ha tenido usted moretones en la piel?
ah te-nee-tho oos-teth mo-re-to-nes en
la pyel

Have you had hives or wheals?

¿Ha tenido usted urticaria (manchas
rojas con comezón) o ampollas con
comezón?
ah te-nee-tho oos-teth oor-tee-ka-rya
(man-chas ro-has con ko-me-son) o
am-po-lyas con ko-me-son

GENERAL NERVOUS SYSTEM

SISTEMA NERVIOSO EN GENERAL
Sees-te-ma ner-vyo-so en he-ne-ral

Have you been irritable?
¿Se ha sentido usted irritable?
se ah sen-tee-tho oos-teth ee-ree-ta-ble

Have you been nervous?
¿Se ha sentido usted nervioso(a) (fem.)
se ah sen-tee-tho oos-teth ner-vyo-so(a)

Do you have headaches?
¿Tiene usted dolores de cabeza?
tye-ne oos-teth do-lo-res de ka-be-sa

Have you had any paralysis?
¿Ha sufrido usted de parálisis?
ah soo-free-do oos-teth de pa-ra-lee-sees

Have you had any dizzines?
¿Ha tenido usted vértigo a veces?
ah te-nee-tho oos-teth ver-tee-go a ve-ses

Have you ever been unconscious?
¿Perdió usted alguna vez el conocimien-to?
per-dyo oos-teth al-goo-na ves el co-no-see-myen-to

When did you notice your condition?
¿Cuándo notó usted su condición?
kwan-do no-to oos-teth soo con-dee-syon

Did you meet with an accident?
¿Tuvo algún accidente?
too-vo al-goon ak-see-den-te

Show me where you have trouble?
¿Enséñeme dónde está el trastorno?
en-seh-nee-me don-deh es-ta el tras-tor-no

Did you develop paralysis?
¿Se paralizó usted?
seh pa-ra-lee-so oos-teth

Were you unconcious or just fainted?
¿Estuvo usted inconciente o se desmayó?
es-too-vo oos-teth een-con-syen-te o se des-ma-yo

How long were you unconscious or fainted?
¿Cuánto tiempo estuvo usted inconciente o desmayado?
kwan-to tyem-po es-too-vo oos-teth een-con-syen-te o des-ma-ya-do

Is this your first time having this condition?
¿Es esta la primera vez que tiene esta condición?
es es-ta la pree-meh-rah vez ke tye-neh es-ta con-dee-syon

How many times did you have it?	¿Cuántas veces la ha tenido? kwan-tas ve-ces la ah teh-nee-tho
When was the last time?	¿Cuándo fué la última vez? kwan-tho foo-eh la ool-tee-ma vez
When this happen, do you have any special sensation warning you that it is going to happen?	¿Cuando le pasa eso, tiene usted alguna sensación especial que le hace saber que la condición le va a ocurrir? kwan-tho le pa-sa eh-so, tye-ne oos-teth al-goo-na sen-sa-syon es-pe-see-al ke le a-seh sa-ber ke la con-dee-syon le vah ah o-koo-reer
What type of sensations do you have?	¿Qué clase de sensaciones tiene usted? ke cla-seh de sen-sa-syo-nes tye-ne oos-teth
Vertigo or dizziness?	¿Vértigo o mareo? ver-tee-go o ma-reh-o
Tingling?	¿Hormigueo? or-mee-gay-oh
Numbness?	¿Adormecimiento? ah-dor-meh-see-myen-to
Pain?	¿Dolor? do-lor
Tenderness?	¿Adolorecimiento? ah-do-lo-reh-see-myen-to
Cold or hot?	¿Frío o caliente? free-oh o ka-lee-en-teh
Sensitive?	¿Sensitividad? sen-see-tee-vee-thad
Weakness?	¿Debilidad? deh-bee-lee-thad
Headaches?	¿Dolores de cabeza? do-lo-res de ca-beh-sa
Double vision?	¿Doble visión? do-bleh vee-syon
Do you see colors around things?	¿Vé colores alrededor de las cosas? veh co-lo-res al-reh-deh-dor de las ko-sas
Blurring of vision?	¿Ofuscación de la vista? oh-foos-ka-syon de la vees-ta

Severe pains inside the eyes?

¿Dolores fuertes dentro de los ojos?
do-lo-res foo-ehr-tes den-tro de los
o-hos

Spots in front of your eyes?

¿Vé manchas o puntos en frente de sus
ojos?
veh man-chas o poon-tos en-fren-te de
soos o-hos

Is your vision all right?

¿Tiene usted buena vista?
tye-ne oos-teth bwe-na vees-ta

Do you use eyeglasses?

¿Usa espejuelos?
oo-sah es-peh-hoo-eh-los

Do you hear well?

¿Oye bien?
o-ee-eh byen

Do you have insomnia or sleep well?

¿Sufre de insomnio or duerme bien?
soo-fre de een-som-nee-oh o doo-er-me
bee-en

Do you keep your balance?

¿Conserva su equilibrio?
con-ser-vah soo eh-kee-lee-bree-o

Do you suffer of convulsions?

¿Sufre de convulsiones?
soo-free de con-vool-syo-nes

What aggravates or alleviates your
condition?

¿Qué agrava o alivia su condición?
keh ah-gra-va o ah-lee-vee-ah soo
con-dee-syon

Have you been treated before?

¿Ha sido tratado antes?
ah see-doh trah-tah-tho an-tes
¿Ha sido tratada antes? (feminine)
ah see-doh trah-tah-tha an-tes

With medicines, or with
injections or electrical shock?

¿Con medicinas, o con inyecciones o
con choques eléctricos?
kon meh-dee-see-nas, o con een-jek-syo-
nes, o con cho-kehs eh-lek-tree-kos

Is there anything wrong with your
sense of taste?

¿Hay algo irregular en su sentido del
gusto?
ay al-go ee-re-goo-lar en su sen-tee-
tho del goos-to

Do you have any discharge from the
ears?

¿Tiene a veces secreciones en las
orejas?
tye-ne a ve-ces se-cre-syo-nes en las
o-re-has

GASTRO-INTESTINAL SYSTEM	SISTEMA GASTRO-INTESTINAL
	Sees-teh-ma gas-tro-een-tes-tee-nal

Is your appetite good?

¿Tiene buen apetito?
tye-ne bwen ah-peh-tee-to

Do you belch a lot?

¿Eructa usted mucho?
e-rook-ta oos-teth moo-cho

Do you have nausea or desire to
vomit?

¿Tiene nausea o ganas de vomitar?
tye-ne naoo-se-ah o ga-nas de vo-mee-
tar

Do you vomit?

¿Vomita usted?
voh-mee-tah oos-teth

Do you ever vomit blood?

¿Vomita usted sangre a veces?
vo-mee-tah oos-teth san-greh a ve-ces

Do you have discomfort of the stomach
after you eat?

¿Siente usted malestar en el estómago
después de comer?
syen-te oos-teth mah-les-tar en el es-
to-mah-go des-poo-es de koh-mer

Do you have pain in the stomach?

¿Tiene dolor en el estómago?
tye-ne do-lor en el es-to-ma-go

Do you have constipation?

¿Está estreñido?
¿Está constipado?
es-ta es-tre-nee-tho
es-ta cons-tee-pah-tho
¿Está estreñida? (femimine)
¿Está constipada? (feminine)
es-ta es-tre-nee-tha
es-ta cons-tee-pah-tha

Do you have diarrhea?

¿Tiene usted diarrea?
tye-ne oos-teth dya-reh-ah

Do you ever have blood in the stool?

¿Ha tenido alguna vez sangre en su
escremento?
ah te-nee-tho al-goo-na ves san-greh en
soo es-cre-men-to

| RESPIRATORY SYSTEM | SISTEMA RESPIRATORIO |
| | Sees-teh-ma res-pee-rah-toh-ree-o |

Do you have any pain in the chest?

¿ Tiene usted algún dolor en el pecho?
tye-ne oos-teth al-goon do-lor en el pe-cho

Do you have a cough?

¿ Tiene tos?
tye-ne tos

Do you bring up sputum with the cough?

¿ Tiene expectoración al toser?
tye-ne ex-pek-to-ra-syon al to-ser

Does the sputum has a foul odor?

¿ Tiene la expectoración mal olor?
tye-ne la ex-pek-to-ra-syon mal o-lor

Is there any blood in the sputum?

¿ Tiene sangre en la expectoración?
tye-ne san-greh en la ex-pek-to-ra-syon

Do you get frequent colds and coughs?

¿ Le dan resfriados y tos frecuentemente?
le dan res-frya-thos ee tos fre-kwen-te-men-te

CIRCULATORY SYSTEM

SISTEMA CIRCULATORIO
Sees-teh-ma seer-koo-lah-toh-ree-o

Do you have shortness of breath?

¿Tiene corta la respiración?
tye-ne cor-ta la res-pee-ra-syon

How many pillows do you sleep on
at night?

¿Cuántas almohadas usa para dormir
en la noche?
kwan-tas al-mo-ah-thas oo-sa pa-ra
dor-meer en la no-che

Do your ankles ever swell up?

¿Se le hinchan los tobillos?
se le een-chan los to-bee-lyos

Do both ankles swell up equally, or
does one get more swollen than the
other?

¿Se le hinchan igualmente los dos tobillos, o uno se hincha mas que el otro?
se le een-chan ee-gwal-men-te los dos
to-bee-lyos, o oo-no se een-cha mas ke
ehl o-tro

Do you ever get a blue color to your
skin, especially around the finger
nails and lips?

¿Se le pone azul la piel alguna vez,
especialmente alrededor de las uñas o
labios?
se le poh-ne a-sool la pyel al-goo-na vez
es-pe-syal-men-te al-re-deh-dor de las
oo-nee-as o la-byos

Do you ever feel that your heart is
boreying away in your chest?

¿Siente a veces que el corazón le golpea
fuertemente en el pecho?
syen-te ah ve-ses ke el co-ra-zon le gol-
pe-ah fwer-te-men-te en el pe-cho

Do you get any pain in front of your
heart?

¿Siente algún dolor sobre el corazón?
syen-te al-goon-do-lor so-bre el co-ra-
son

Do you have to jump up while in bed
at night to catch your breath?

¿Se ve obligado (a) a sentarse de repen-
te mientras está en cama para poder
respirar?
se ve o-blee-ga-tho (tha) ah sen-tar-se
de re-pen-te myen-tras es-ta en ka-ma
pa-ra po-ther res-pee-rar

Do you know if you have high blood
pressure?

¿Sabe si tiene presión alta de sangre?
sa-be see tye-ne pre-syon al-ta de sangre

Can you breathe comfortably if you
only have one pillow?

¿Puede respirar cómodamente si usa
una sola almohada?
pwe-de res-pee-rar co-mo-da-men-te
see oo-sa oo-na so-la al-mo-ah-tha

URINARY SYSTEM

SISTEMA URINARIO
Sees-teh-ma oo-ree-nah-ryo

Do you ever have any pain when
you urinate?

¿Al orinar siente usted algún dolor?
al o-ree-nar syen-te oos-teth al-goon
do-lor

Do you ever have blood in the urine?

¿Ha visto usted alguna vez sangre en la
orina?
ah vees-to oos-teth al-goo-na vez san-
greh en la o-ree-nah

Do you have to urinate a great many
times a day?

¿Tiene usted que orinar muchísimas
veces al día?
tye-ne oos-teth ke o-ree-nar mu-chee-
see-mas ve-ces al dee-a

Do you have to get up at night to
urinate? How many times?

¿Tiene usted que levantarse durante la
noche para orinar? ¿Cuántas veces?
tye-ne oos-teth ke le-vahn-tar-se doo-
ran-te la noh-che pa-ra o-ree-nar
kwan-tas ve-ses

Does it take you a long time to
start to urinate?

¿Le requiere a usted mucho tiempo para
empezar a orinar?
le re-kye-re ah oos-teth moo-cho tyem-
po pa-ra em-peh-sar ah o-ree-nar

Do you often have the feeling that you
have to urinate very badly?

¿Le vienen con frequencia muchas ganas
de orinar urgentemente?
le vye-nen con fre-kwen-see-a moo-chas
ga-nas de o-ree-nar oor-hen-te-men-te

Do you have any leaking of the urine
unintentionally?

¿Gotea orina involuntariamente algunas
veces?
go-te-ah o-ree-na een-vo-loon-ta-rya-
men-te al-goo-nas ve-ses

Is it worse when you cough or sneeze?

¿Gotea más cuando tose o estornuda?
go-te-ah mas kwan-do toh-se o es-tor-
noo-tha

Do you ever have narrowing of the
stream of urine?

¿Ha tenido usted alguna vez disminución
en el calibre del chorro de la orina?
ah te-nee-do oos-teth al-goo-na ves
dees-mee-noo-syon en el ka-lee-breh
del cho-rroh de la o-ree-na

Do you know if you ever had sugar
in the urine?

¿Sabe usted si ha tenido azúcar en la
orina?
sa-beh oos-teth see ah te-nee-do a-zoo-
car en la o-ree-na

Did somebody hit you?

¿Alguien le pegó?
al-gee-en le peh-go

Did somebody kick you?

¿Le dió alguien alguna patada (o punta-pie)?
le dee-o al-gee-en al-goo-na pa-ta-da (o poon-ta-pye)

Did you fall down?

¿Se cayó usted?
se ka-yo oos-teth

Were you drunk?

¿Estaba usted tomado o ebrio?
es-ta-ba oos-teth to-ma-tho o e-bree-o (tomada o ebria - feminine)
to-ma-tha o e-bree-a

Did you ever have urine looking like milk?

¿Tuvo alguna vez orina del color de la leche?
too-vo al-goo-na ves o-ree-na del ko-lor de la leh-che

What is the color of the urine? Dark or light?

¿Cuál es el color de la orina? ¿Oscura o clara?
kwal es el ko-lor de la o-ree-na os-koo-ra o kla-ra

Did you ever had sand or stones in the urine?

¿Tuvo alguna vez arena o piedras en la orina?
too-vo al-goo-na ves a-re-na o pee-e-dras en la o-ree-na

Has the urine a white or reddish sediment?

¿Tiene la orina sedimento blanco o rojizo?
tye-ne la o-ree-na se-dee-men-to blan-ko o ro-hee-so

Do you have burning urination?

¿Tiene la orina quemante?
tye-ne la o-ree-na ke-man-te

Do you have threads or mucus like pieces floating in the urine?

¿Tiene hilos o pedazos de moco flotando en la orina?
tye-ne ee-los o pe-da-sos de mo-co flo-tan-tho en la o-ree-na

Do you have pains at the end of urination?

¿Tiene dolores al acabar de orinar?
tye-ne do-lo-res al a-ca-bar de o-ree-nar

Is the urinary flow interrupted?

¿Es el chorro urinario interrumpido?
es el cho-rro oo-ree-na-ryo een-te-room-pee-do

VENEREAL HISTORY

HISTORIA VENEREA
Ees-to-rya ve-neh-reh-ah

What venereal diseases did you have?

¿Qué enfermedades venéreas tuvo
usted?
ke en-fer-meh-dah-des ve-neh-reh-as
too-vo oos-teth

Gonorrhea?

¿Gonorrea?
go-no-reh-ah

Syphilis?

¿Sífilis?
see-fee-lees

Chancre?

¿Chancro?
chan-cro

When?

¿Cuándo?
kwan-do

Were you treated?

¿Tuvo usted tratamiento?
too-vo oos-teth tra-tah-myen-to

How were you treated?

¿Qué tratamiento le dieron?
ke tra-ta-myen-to le dye-ron

Did you get injections?

¿Le dieron inyecciones?
le dye-ron een-jek-syo-nes

MENSTRUAL HISTORY

HISTORIA MENSTRUAL
Ees-to-rya mens-troo-al

How old were you when you started
to menstruate?

¿A qué edad empezó usted a menstruar?
ah ke eh-thad em-peh-so oos-teth ah
mens-troo-ar

How many days are there from one
period of bleeding to the next?

¿Cuántos días entre cada periodo?
kwan-tos dy-as en-tre ca-da pe-ryo-tho

Is the interval between your periods
always regular?

¿Es el intervalo entre los periodos
siempre regular?
es el een-ter-va-lo en-tre los pe-ryo-
thos syem-pre re-goo-lar

How long does the blood flow last
during each period?

¿Cuánto tiempo le dura cada periodo?
kwan-to tyem-po le doo-ra ca-tha pe-
ryo-do

Is there a great deal, a small amount,
or moderate amount of bleeding?

¿Es mucha, o poca o moderada la cantidad de sangre?
es moo-cha, o po-ka, o mo-the-rah-dah
la kan-tee-dad de san-greh

When was your last period?

¿Cuándo fué su último periodo?
kwan-tho foo-eh soo ool-tee-mo pe-ryo-
tho

When was the period before that last
one?

¿Cuándo fué el penúltimo periodo?
kwan-tho foo-eh el pe-nool-tee-mo
pe-ryo-tho

Is your menstrual period overdue?

¿Está atrasada, al presente?
es-tah ah-trah-sah-tha al pre-sen-te

Did you have any pain during the
bleeding?

¿Siente usted algún dolor durante la
menstruación?
syen-teh oos-teth al-goon do-lor doo-
ran-te la mens-troo-ah-syon

Before?

¿Antes?
ahn-tes

After?

¿Después?
des-pwes

Do you have any discharge other than
blood from down below?

¿Tiene usted algún derrame o secreción
además de sangre por sus partes privadas (o vagina)?
tye-ne oos-teth al-goon der-rah-meh,
o seh-creh-syon ah-de-mas de san-greh
por soos par-tes pree-va-thas (o va-
hee-nah)

When the last time you had
intercourse?

¿Cuándo fué la última vez que tuvo relaciones sexuales?
kwan-tho foo-eh la ool-tee-ma ves keh
too-vo reh-lah-syo-nes sek-soo-ah-les

Do you think it is possible that you
are now pregnant?

¿Cree usted que sea posible que esté
en estado (o embarazada)?
kreh oos-teh keh seh-ah poh-see-ble keh
es-teh ehn es-tha-tho (o em-bah-rah-sa-
tha)

What is the color of your menstrual
blood?

¿Cuál es el color de su sangre
menstrual?
kwal es el co-lor de soo san-gre mens-
troo-ahl

- Red

Roja
ro-ha

- Dark red

Roja oscura
ro-ha os-koo-rah

- Light red

Roja clara
ro-ha cla-rah

- Blood tinged

Rosada
ro-sah-that

- Chocolate

Chocolate
cho-ko-lah-teth

Do you pass large blood clots?

¿Pasa usted coágulos de sangre muy
grandes?
pa-sah oos-teth kwa-goo-los de san-
greh mooy gran-des

Did you have a miscarriage?
(An abortion?)

¿Tuvo aborto accidental o provocado?
too-vo ah-bor-to ak-see-den-tal o
pro-vo-ka-tho

OBSTETRICAL HISTORY	HISTORIA DE OBSTETRICIA ees-to-rya de obs-te-tree-sya
Have you ever been pregnant?	¿Ha estado alguna vez en estado (o embarazada)? ah es-ta-tho al-goo-na ves en es-ta-tho (o em-bah-rah-sah-tha)
How many times have you been pregnant?	¿Cuántas veces ha estado en estado? kwan-tas ve-ses ah es-ta-tho en es-ta-tho
Have you had any miscarriages, accidental or on purpose?	¿Ha tenido abortos accidentales o a propósito? ah te-nee-tho ah-bor-tos ak-see-den-ta-les o ah pro-po-see-to
When did you have a miscarriage?	¿Cuándo tuvo el aborto? kwan-tho too-vo el ah-bor-to
How many months were you pregnant when you had the miscarriage?	¿Cuántos meses tenía el embarazo cuando tuvo el aborto? Kwan-tos meh-ses te-nya el em-bah-rah-so kwan-tho too-vo el ah-bor-to
How many children have you had?	¿Cuántas criaturas ha tenido? Kwan-tas cree-ah-too-ras ah te-nee-tho
Was the first pregnancy normal?	¿Fué normal su primer embarazo? foo-eh nor-mal soo pree-mer em-bah-rah-so
First	Primer (o primero) pree-mer (o pree-meh-ro
Second	Segundo seh-goon-do
Third	Tercero ter-seh-ro
Fourth	Cuarto kwar-to
Fifth	Quinto keen-to
Sixth	Sexto sek-to
Seventh	Séptimo sep-tee-mo

| Eighth | Octavo
ok-ta-vo |

Ninth

Noveno
no-veh-no

Tenth

Décimo
deh-see-mo

Was the labor normal for the last child?

¿Fué su último parto normal?
foo-eh soo ool-tee-mo par-to nor-mal

Was the labor long?

¿Fueron los dolores de parto prolongados?
foo-he-ron los do-lo-res de par-to pro-lon-ga-thos

Were you sick after the baby was delivered?

¿Se enfermó después que la criatura nació?
se en-fer-mo des-pwes ke la cree-ah-too-rah nah-syo

Did the doctor have to use instruments to deliver the baby?

¿Tuvo el doctor la necesidad de usar instrumentos para el nacimiento de la criatura?
too-vo el dok-tor la neh-seh-see-thad de oo-sar eens-troo-men-tos pa-ra el nah-see-myen-to de la cree-ah-too-rah

How many pounds did the baby weigh at birth?

¿Cuántas libras pesó la criatura al nacer?
kwan-tas lee-bras pe-so la cree-ah-too-rah al nah-ser

Did you ever get swollen ankles during pregnancy?

¿Se le han hinchado los tobillos alguna vez durante el embarazo?
se le ahn een-cha-tho los to-bee-lyos al-goo-na ves doo-ran-teh el em-bah-rah-so

Did you ever get large veins on your legs during pregnancy?

¿Ha tenido venas prominentes durante el embarazo?
ah te-nee-tho veh-nas pro-mee-nen-tes doo-ran-te el em-bah-rah-so

Did you ever get high blood pressure during pregnancy?

¿Tuvo alguna vez presión alta de sangre durante el embarazo?
too-vo al-goo-na ves pre-syon al-ta de san-greh doo-ran-te el em-bah-rah-so

Did you ever get kidney troubles, or
convulsions during pregnancy?

¿Tuvo alguna vez, durante su embarazo,
mal de riñones o convulsiones?
too-vo al-goo-na ves, doo-ran-te soo
em-bah-rah-so mal de ree-nyoh-nes o
con-vool-syo-nes

Was each baby alive at birth?

¿Nació cada criatura viva?
nah-syo ca-da cree-ah-too-rah vee-vah

How much did the first baby weight?

¿Cuánto pesó la primera criatura?
kwan-to peh-so la pree-meh-ra cree-
ah-too-rah

Did you have eye disturbances during
pregnancy?

¿Tuvo disturbios de la vista durante el
embarazo?
too-vo dees-toor-byos deh la vees-tah
doo-ran-teh el em-bah-rah-so

- Blurring

Ofuscación
o-foos-ka-syon

- Colors

Colores
ko-lo-res

- Pains

Dolores
do-lo-res

- Spots - fixed or moving

Manchas - fijas o movibles
man-chas fee-has o mo-vee-blays

HISTORY OF THE PRESENT PREGNANCY	HISTORIA DEL PRESENTE EMBARAZO ees-to-rya del preh-sen-teh em-bah-rah-so
What was the date of your last normal period?	¿Cuál fué la fecha de su última menstruación normal? kwal foo-eh la fe-cha de soo ool-tee-ma mens-troo-ah-syon nor-mal
Have you had dizziness?	¿Tuvo vértigo o mareo? too-vo ver-tee-go o ma-reh-o
- persistent headaches?	-dolores de cabeza? do-lo-res de ca-be-sa
- disturbed vision?	-disturbios de la vista? dees-toor-byos de la vees-tah
- shortness of breath?	-cortedad de respiración? kor-te-thad de res-pee-ra-syon
- annoying heart beatings?	-palpitaciones que la molestaron? pal-pee-tah-syo-nes keh la mo-les-tah-ron
- nausea?	-náusea nah-oo-seh-ah
- vomiting?	-vómitos vo-mee-tos
- enlargement of the breast with tenderness?	- crecimiento de los senos, con dolor? cre-see-myen-to de los seh-nos, kon do-lor
- diarrhea?	-diarrea? dee-ah-reh-ah
- constipation?	-constipación o estreñimiento? kons-tee-pa-syon o es-tre-nee-myen-to
-any vaginal discharge?	-algún derrame o descarga vaginal? al-goon deh-rah-me o des-kar-gah vah-he-nal
- bleeding from the vagina?	-sangrando vaginalmente? san-gran-tho vah-hee-nal-men-teh

Have you put anything into the vagina or womb?

¿Ha puesto usted algo dentro de la vagina o matriz?
ah pwes-to oos-teth al-go den-tro de la va-he-na o mah-treeth

-Why?

¿Por qué?
por keh

Have you had to urinate frequently?

¿Ha tenido que orinar frecuentemente?
ah te-nee-tho ke o-ree-nar freh-kwen-teh-men-teh

Have your ankles swollen up?

¿Se le han hinchado los tobillos?
se le ahn een-cha-tho los to-bee-lyos

Have your hands swollen up?

¿Se le han hinchado las manos?
se le ahn een-cha-tho las mah-nos

Have your face swollen up?

¿Se le ha hinchado la cara?
se le ah een-cha-tho la kah-rah

Have you had any cramps in the legs?

¿Ha tenido calambres en las piernas?
ah te-nee-tho cah-lam-bres en las pyer-nas

Have you had any of the following diseases and at what age?

¿Ha sufrido usted de algunas de las siguientes enfermedades, y a qué edad?
ah soo-free-tho oos-teth de al-goo-nas de la see-gyen-tes en-fer-meh-tha-thes ee a keh e-thad

- Scarlet Fever

-Escarlatina
es-kar-la-tee-nah

- Diphtheria

-Difteria
deef-te-ree-ah

- Measles

- Sarampión
sa-ram-pyon

- Tonsillitis

- Tonsilitis o amigdalitis
ton-see-lee-tees o ah-meeg-dah-lee-tees

- Mumps

- Paperas, o farfallotas o parótidas
pah-pe-ras, o far-fah-lyo-tas o pah-roh-tee-das

- Rheumatic Fever

- Fiebre reumática
fye-bre ray-oo-mah-tee-ka

- Tuberculosis

- Tuberculosis
too-ber-coo-lo-sees

- Typhoid Fever

- Frequent "colds"

- Convulsive seizures

- Nervous breakdown

- Pneumonia

- Heart disease

- Kidney disease

- Syphilis

- Gonorrhea

- Any other venereal disease

- Any other disease

Is there any of the following diseases in any member of your immediate family?

- Tuberculosis

- Heart disease

- Diabetes

- Cancer

- Fiebre tifoidea
fye-bre tee-foy-day-ah

-Frecuentes resfriados
fray-kwen-tes res-free-ah-thos

Ataques de convulsiones
ah-ta-kehs de con-vool-syo-nes

-Postración de nervios
pos-tra-syon de ner-vyos

- Pulmonía
pool-mo-nya

- Enfermedades del corazón
en-fehr-me-tha-des del ko-rah-son

- Enfermedad de los riñones
en-fehr-me-thad de los ree-nyo-nes

- Sífilis
see-fee-lees

- Gonorrea
go-no-reh-ah

- Cualquiera otra enfermedad venérea
koo-al-kee-eh-rah o-tra en-fehr-me-
thad ve-neh-reh-ah

- Cualquiera otra enfermedad
koo-al-kee-eh-rah o-tra en-fer-me-
thad

¿Entre los miembros de su inmediata
familia ha tenido alguien alguna de las
siguientes enfermedades?
en-treh los myem-bros de soo een-meh-
dya-ta fah-mee-lya ah teh-nee-tho al-
gee-ehn al-goo-nah de las see-gee-ehn-
tes en-fehr-me-tha-des

- Tuberculosis
too-behr-coo-lo-sees

- Enfermedad del corazón
en-fehr-me-thad del ko-rah-son

- Diabetes
dya-be-tes

- Cancer
kan-ser

- Stroke	- Parálisis repentina pa-rah-lee-sees re-pen-tee-na
- Obesity (fat)	- Obesidad (gordura) o-be-see-thad (gor-doo-rah)
- High blood pressure	- Alta presión de sangre ahl-tah pre-syon de san-greh
- Blood disease	- Enfermedad de la sangre en-fehr-me-thad de la san-greh
Is your mother alive?	¿Vive su madre? vee-ve soo ma-dreh
- Father	Padre pah-dreh
- Sister	- Hermana ehr-ma-nah
- Brother	- Hermano ehr-ma-noh
- Son	- Hijo ee-ho
- Daughter	- Hija ee-ha
- Husband	- Marido ma-ree-tho
- Wife	- Esposa o mujer es-po-sah o moo-her
What was the cause of death?	¿Cuál fué la causa de su muerte? kwal foo-eh la ka-oo-sa de soo moo-ehr-teh
At what age did he die?	¿A qué edad murió él? ah ke eh-thad moo-ree-o ehl
At what age did she die?	¿A qué edad murió ella? ah ke eh-thad moo-ree-o eh-ya
Have you ever had any surgical operation?	¿Ha tenido usted alguna operación quirúrgica? ah te-nee-tho oos-teth al-goo-na o-peh-rah-syon kee-roor-gee-ka

For what condition were you
operated on?

¿Por qué condición le hicieron la
operación?
por keh kon-dee-syon le ee-see-eh-ron
la o-peh-ra-syon

At what age did you have the operation?

¿A qué edad tuvo la operación?
ah keh e-thad too-vo la o-peh-ra-syon

FAMILY HISTORY

HISTORIA DE LA FAMILIA
ees-toh-ree-ah de la fa-mee-lee-ah

Have you had among the family or
ancestors the following?:

¿Ha tenido entre la familia o predece-
sores lo siguiente?:
ah te-nee-tho en-tre la fah-mee-lya o
pre-the-seh-so-rehs lo see-gee-ehn-te

- Headaches?

¿Dolores de cabeza?
do-lo-res de ca-beh-sa

- Epilepsy?

¿Epilepsia?
eh-pee-lep-see-ah

- Abnormal motions?

¿Movimientos abnormales?
mo-vee-myen-tos ab-nor-ma-les

- Deviations of the eye balls?

¿Desviaciones de los ojos?
des-vee-ah-syo-nes de los o-hos

- Muscular atrophy?

¿Desgaste de los músculos?
des-gas-te de los moos-koo-los

- Difficulty in walking?

¿Dificultad en caminar?
dee-fee-kool-thad en ca-mee-nar

- Neuralgias or neuritis?

¿Neuralgias o neuritis?
neh-oo-ral-hee-as o neh-oo-ree-tees

- Mental retardation?

¿Pobre desarrollo mental?
po-bre deh-sar-ro-lyo men-tal

- Insanity?

¿Locura?
lo-koo-rah

SOCIAL HISTORY

HISTORIA SOCIAL
ees-to-ree-ah so-see-al

Are you married or single?

¿Está usted casada, o es soltera?
es-tah oos-teth kah-sah-tha, o es sol-
teh-ra
¿Está usted casado, o es soltero?
(masculine)
es-tah oos-teth kah-sah-tho, o es sol-
teh-ro

Do you live with your husband?

¿Vive usted con su marido?
vee-ve oos-teth con soo mah-ree-tho

Do you live with your wife?

¿Vive usted con su esposa?
vee-ve oos-teth con soo es-po-sah

What is the name of the father of your
child?

¿Cómo se llama el padre de su criatura?
ko-mo seh lya-mah el pah-dreh de soo
cree-ah-too-rah

Do you work or do you stay at home?

¿Trabaja usted o se queda en casa?
trah-bah-ha oos-teth o seh keh-tha en
kah-sa

Do you smoke?

¿Fuma usted?
foo-mah oos-teth

Do you drink alcoholic beverages?

¿Toma usted bebidas alcóholicas?
to-mah oos-teth beh-bee-thas al-ko-
lee-cas

Do you drink a great deal of coffee?

¿Bebe usted mucho café?
beh-be oos-teth moo-cho ka-feh

Do you take any narcotics or drugs
from habit?

¿Tiene usted el vicio de tomar narcóticos o drogas?
tye-ne oos-teth el vee-syo de to-mar
nar-co-tee-cos o dro-gas

How many rooms are there in your
apartment?

¿Cuántos cuartos tiene su apartamento?
kwan-tos kwar-tos tye-ne soo ah-par-
tah-men-to

How many people live in the same
apartment with you?

¿Cuántas personas viven en el mismo
apartamento con usted?
kwan-tas per-so-nas vee-ven en el
mees-mo ah-par-tah-men-to con
oos-teth

Are you pleased with your work?

¿Está usted contento (a) con su trabajo?
es-tah oos-teth con-ten-to (a) con soo
trah-bah-ho
    contenta - feminine

What education have you had?

¿Qué educación ha tenido usted?
ke eh-doo-ca-syon ah te-nee-tho oos-
teh

How is your marital life?

¿Cómo anda su vida matrimonial?
co-mo an-tha soo vee-dah ma-tree-mo-
nee-al

How are your children behaving?

¿Cómo se portan sus hijos?
co-mo se por-tan soos ee-hos

Do you have many friends?

¿Tiene muchos amigos?
tye-ne moo-chos ah-mee-gos
   (amigas - feminine)

Do you belong to some club, society,
or church?

¿Es miembro de algún club, sociedad
o parroquia?
es myem-bro de al-goon cloob, so-sye-
thad, o par-ro-kya

THE PSYCHIATRIC HISTORY
        IN DETAIL

What is your complaint?

Tell me everything about your
complaint

When did it start?

How often?

How long does it last?

When did you have it last?

Have you a good memory?

Have you any fears?

Do you become aggresive at times?

Do you see imaginary persons,
animals or things?

Do you hear voices?

Do you hear unusual sounds?

Have you fears of persecution?

Do you have a normal sex life?

HISTORIA PSIQUIATRICA
ees-to-ree-ah see-kee-ah-tree-kah

¿Cuál es su queja?
kwal es soo ke-ha

Dígame todo acerca de su queja
dee-ga-meh to-do ah-ser-ca de soo
ke-ha

¿Cuándo comenzó?
kwan-tho co-men-so

¿Qué tan amenudo?
ke tan ah-me-noo-do

¿Cuánto le dura?
kwan-to le doo-rah

¿Cuándo lo tuvo por última vez?
kwan-do lo too-vo por ool-tee-mah ves

¿Tiene buena memoria?
tye-ne boo-eh-nah me-mo-rya

¿Tiene miedos de alguna clase?
tye-ne mee-eh-dos de al-goo-na cla-se

¿Le dan deseos de atacar personas o
destruir cosas?
le dan de-seh-os de ah-ta-kar per-so-
nas o des-troo-eer co-sas

¿Vé usted personas, animales, o cosas
imaginarias?
veh oos-teth per-so-nas, ah-nee-mah-
les, o co-sas ee-mah-hee-nah-ree-as

¿Oye usted voces?
o-yeh oos-teth vo-ses

¿Oye usted sonidos raros?
o-yeh oos-teth so-nee-dos ra-ros

¿Tiene usted miedos que lo persiguen?
tye-ne oos-teth myeh-dos ke lo per-see-
gehn

¿Tiene usted una vida sexual normal?
tye-ne oos-teth oo-na vee-da sek-soo-al
nor-mal

Do you have satisfaction with the same or opposite sex?

¿Tiene usted satisfacción con el mismo sexo o el opuesto?
tye-ne oos-teth sah-tees-fak-syon con el mees-mo sek-so o el o-pwes-to

Do you satisfy yourself with masturbation?

¿Se satisface usted mismo con masturbación?
seh sa-tees-fa-se oos-teth mees-mo (mees-mah - feminine) con mas-toor-ba-syon

Have you spells of convulsions?

¿Tiene ataques de convulciones?
tye-ne ah-ta-kes de con-vool-syo-nes

Do you have body or mental disturbances often or constantly?

¿Tiene usted disturbios corporales muy a menudo o constantemente?
tye-ne oos-teth dees-toor-bee-os cor-po-ra-les moo-ee ah me-noo-do o constan-teh-men-teh

Do you feel weak or mentally depressed often?

¿Se siente usted débil o mentalmente decaído?
se syen-teh oos-teth deh-beel o mental-men-teh deh-ka-ee-do

Do you worry thinking you have a serious illness?

¿Se aflije creyendo que tiene alguna enfermedad mala?
se ah-flee-he cre-yen-do ke tye-ne al-goo-nah en-fer-meh-thad mah-lah

Do you have fainting spells?

¿Tiene ataques de desmayo?
tye-ne ah-tah-kes de des-ma-yo

Are you very apprehensive?

¿Es usted muy aprensivo(a) female
Es oos-teth moo-ee a-pren-see-vo

Do you suffer of insomnia?

¿Sufre de insomnio?
soo-fre de een-som-nyo

Do you take narcotics, drugs, or sedatives?

¿Usa narcóticos, drogas, o sedativos?
oo-sah nar-ko-tee-kos, dro-gas o seh-dah-tee-vos

How much coffe and tea do you take a day?

¿Cuánto café y té toma al día?
kwan-to ka-feh ee teh to-ma al dya

How much alcohol, wine, and beer do you drink a day?

¿Cuánto alcohol, vino, y cerveza bebe al día?
kwan-to al-co-ol vee-no ee ser-veh-sa beh-be al dya

How much do you smoke a day?

¿Cuánto fuma al día?
kwan-to foo-mah al dya

Are you happy at your work?	¿Está contento (a)(feminine) en el tra-bajo? es-tah con-ten-to (a) en el trah-bah-ho
Have you many friends among your co-workers?	¿Tiene usted muchos amigos (as)(female) entre sus compañeros (as)(female) de trabajo? tye-ne oos-teth moo-chos ah-mee-gos (ah-mee-gas) en-treh soos com-pah-nye-ros (ras) de trah-bah-ho
Do you get along well with your relatives and friends?	¿Está en buenas relaciones con sus familiares y amigos (as)(female)? es-tah en boo-eh-nas re-la-syo-nes con soos fah-mee-lya-res ee ah-mee-gos (ah-mee-gas)
What kind of sports, entertainments or hobbies do you like?	¿Qué clase de deportes, entretenimien-to, o cosas le gustan más? ke clah-seh de deh-por-tes, en-tre-teh-nee-myen-to, o ko-sas le goos-tan mas
Any maladjustments in infancy?	¿Algunos malos hábitos en la infancia? al-goo-nos mah-los ah-bee-tos en la een-fan-see-ah
Did you bite the finger nails?	¿Se mordía las uñas de los dedos? se mor-dya las oo-nee-as de los de-dos
Did you suck your thumb?	¿Se chupaba el dedo pulgar (o gordo)? se choo-pah-bah el deh-do pool-gar (o gor-do)
Were you afraid of storms, animals or other things?	¿Le tenía miedo a las tormentas, ani-males u otras cosas? le te-nya mee-eh-do a las tor-men-tas, ah-nee-mah-les oo o-tras ko-sas
Were you finicky with the food?	¿Era usted muy particular con sus alimentos? eh-ra oos-teth moo-ee par-tee-koo-lar con soos ah-lee-men-tos
Were you contented in school?	¿Estaba contento (a) female en la es-cuela? es-tah-ba con-ten-to (ta) en la es-kwe-la
Did you get good marks, and engaged in sports?	¿Tenía buenas notas y tomaba parte en los deportes? te-nya boo-eh-nas no-tas ee to-mah-bah par-teh en los deh-por-tes

Did you lie much?

¿Mentía mucho?
men-tya moo-cho

Did you steal?

¿Robó usted?
ro-boh oos-teth

Did you cut classes?

¿Faltó mucho a las clases?
fal-to moo-cho ah las cla-ses

Did you torment and hit children
and animals?

¿Molestó o maltrató a otras criaturas
o animales?
mo-les-toh o mal-tra-toh ah o-tras
cree-ah-too-ras o ah-nee-mah-les

What kind of jobs did you hold?

¿Qué clase de trabajos hizo usted?
ke cla-se deh trah-bah-hos ee-so
oos-teth

How long did you hold your jobs?

¿Cuánto duró en sus trabajos?
kwan-to doo-roh en soos trah-bah-hos

How much did you get pay?

¿Cuánto le pagaban?
kwan-to le pah-gah-ban

Tell me all the illnesses and operations
that you had?

Dígame las enfermedades y operaciones
que tuvo
dee-gah-me las en-fer-meh-tha-des ee
o-pe-ra-syo-nes ke too-vo

Did you have syphilis, gonorrhea, or
chancre?

¿Tuvo usted sífilis, gonorrea, o
chancro?
too-vo oos-teth see-fee-lees, go-no-
reh-ah, o chan-cro

Do you have many responsibilities?

¿Tiene usted muchas responsibilidades?
tye-ne oos-teth moo-chas res-pon-sah-
bee-lee-dah-des

Do you have any debts?

¿Tiene usted muchas deudas?
tye-ne oos-teth moo-chas deh-oo-das

Do you like to save or spend?

¿Le gusta gastar o ahorrar?
le goos-ta gas-tar o ah-or-rar

Are you religious?

¿Es usted religioso?
es oos-teth reh-lee-hee-o-so

Do you belong to some societies,
clubs, religious organizations or
others?

¿Pertenece a algunas sociedades, clubs,
organizaciones religiosas u otras?
per-teh-neh-se ah al-goo-nas so-sye-
tha-des, cloobs, or-ga-nee-sa-syo-nes
reh-lee-he-o-sas oo o-tras

Among your family, relatives or
ancestors have you had?:

¿Entre su familia, parientes y antecesores ha habido casos de?:
en-treh soo fah-mee-lya, pa-ryen-tes
ee an-teh-seh-so-res ah ah-bee-tho
ca-sos de:

Mental disorders?

¿Desórdenes mentales?
deh-sor-deh-nes men-tah-les

Idiot?

¿Idiotas?
ee-dee-o-tas

Physical abnormalities?

¿Abnormalidades físicas?
ab-nor-mah-lee-dah-des fee-see-cas

Epileptics?

¿Epilépticos?
eh-pee-lep-tee-cos

Alcoholics?

¿Alcohólicos?
al-co-o-lee-cos

Drug addicts?

¿Adictos a drogas?
ah-deek-tos ah dro-gas

Syphilitics?

¿Sifilíticos?
see-fee-lee-tee-cos

Infantile paralysis?

¿Parálisis infantil?
pah-rah-lee-sees een-fan-teel

Feebleminded?

¿Mentalmente trastornados?
men-tal-men-te tras-tor-nah-thos

Maniacs?

¿Maniáticos?
mah-nee-ah-tee-cos

Homosexuals?

¿Homosexuales?
o-mo-sek-soo-ah-les

Interfamilial marriages?

¿Casamientos interfamiliares?
cah-sah-myen-tos een-ter-fah-mee-
lya-res

Any in insane asylum?

¿Alguien en el manicomio?
al-gee-en en el ma-nee-co-mee-o

Any convicted of a crime,
robbery, assault, rape, etc.?

¿Alguien sentenciado por algún crimen,
robo, asalto, rapto, etc.?
al-gyen sen-ten-sya-tho por al-goon
cree-men, ro-bo, ah-sal-to, o rap-to
etc.

QUESTIONS ON MALE INFERTILITY

What is your name?

How old are you?

What is your wife's name?

How old is your wife?

Have you been married before?

Did you have any children by your previous marriage?

Has your wife been married before?

Has your wife had any children by her previous marriage?

Did your wife had an operation to prevent pregnancy?

What is your religion?

What is the religion of your wife?

What is your occupation?

Have you ever worked with x-rays?

PREGUNTAS SOBRE INFERTILIDAD DEL HOMBRE
pre-goon-tas so-bre een-fer-tee-lee-thad del om-breh

¿Cuál es su nombre?
kwal es soo nom-bre

¿Su edad?
soo eh-thad

¿Cuál es el nombre de su esposa?
kwal es el nom-bre de soo es-po-sah

¿Cuál es la edad de su esposa?
kwal es la e-thad de su es-po-sah

¿Se ha casado usted antes?
se ah cah-sah-tho oos-teth an-tes

¿Tiene hijos de su matrimonio anterior?
tye-ne ee-hos de su ma-tree-mo-nyo an-te-ryor

¿Estuvo su esposa casada anterior-mente?
es-too-vo soo es-po-sah cah-sah-tha an-te-ryor-men-te

¿Tiene su esposa hijos de su matrimonio anterior?
tye-ne soo es-po-sah ee-hos de su ma-tree-mo-nyo an-te-ryor

¿Ha sido su señora operada para no tener hijos?
ah see-do soo se-nyo-rah o-peh-rah-da pa-ra no teh-ner ee-hos

¿Cuál es su religión?
kwal es soo reh-lee-hee-on

¿Cuál es la religión de su esposa?
kwal es lah re-lee-hee-on de soo es-po-sah

¿Cuál es su ocupación?
kwal es soo o-coo-pah-syon

¿Ha trabajado usted con rayos x?
ah trah-bah-ha-tho oos-teth con ra-yos eh-kees

For how many years have you been
married?

¿Por cuántos años ha estado casado?
por kwan-tos ah-nyos ah es-ta-tho ca-
sah-do

Have now been any pregnancies?

¿Han ocurrido embarazos en su actual
matrimonio?
an o-coo-ree-do em-bah-rah-sos en soo
ak-twal ma-tree-mo-nyo

How many pregnancies have occurred?

¿Cuántos embarazos han habido?
kwan-tos em-bah-rah-sos an ah-bee-do

Were there miscarriages?

¿Hubo pérdidas de embarazos?
oo-bo per-dee-das de em-bah-rah-sos

Were any children born dead?

¿Alguna de las criaturas nació muerta?
al-goo-na de las cree-ah-too-ras na-syo
moo-er-ta

Were any children born alive but died
quickly?

¿Alguna de las criaturas nació viva
pero murió enseguida?
al-goo-na de las cree-ah-too-ras na-syo
vee-va pe-ro moo-ryo en-seh-gee-dah

How many live children do you have?

¿Cuántas criaturas tiene vivas?
kwan-tas cree-ah-too-ras tye-ne vee-vas

Did you or your wife use any methods
(contraceptives) to prevent pregnancy
for a time after your marriage?

¿Ha usado usted o su esposa algún método (contraceptivo) para prevenir embarazo por algún tiempo después de su
matrimonio?
ah oo-sah-do oos-teth o soo es-po-sah
al-goon meh-to-do (con-tra-sep-tee-
vo) pah-rah preh-veh-neer em-bah-rah-
so por al-goon tyem-po des-pwes de
soo mah-tree-mo-nyo

Does your wife uses any douching
right after intercourse?

¿Usa su esposa duchas enseguida después del contacto sexual?
oo sah soo es-po-sah doo-chas en-seh-
gee-dah des-poo-es del con-tak-to sek-
soo-al

What method of contraception did
you use?

¿Qué método de prevención (contraceptivo) usó usted?
ke meh-to-do de preh-ven-syon (con-
tra-sep-tee-vo) oo-so oos-teth

How long have you been trying to
have a baby?

¿Por cuánto tiempo ha estado tratando
de tener hijos?
por kwan-to tyem-po ah es-tah-do trah-
tan-do de teh-ner ee-hos

Have you been in good general health?

¿Ha estado usted en buena salud en general?
ah es-tah-do oos-teth en boo-eh-na sah-looth en geh-geh-ral

Is your weight steady?

¿Es su peso constante?
es soo peh-so cons-tan-teh

Have you been gaining weight?

¿Está usted ganando peso?
es-tah oos-teth gah-nan-do peh-so

Have you been losing weight?

¿Está usted perdiendo peso?
es-tah oos-teth per-dyen-do peh-so

Do you sleep well?

¿Duerme bien?
doo-er-meh byen

Is your appetite good?

¿Tiene buen apetito?
tye-neh boo-en ah-peh-tee-to

Do you use tobacco? How much?

¿Usa tabaco? ¿Cuánto?
oo-sah tah-bah-ko Kwan-to

Do you drink much alcoholic drinks?

¿Bebe muchas bebidas alcohólicas?
beh-beh moo-chas beh-bee-das al-co-o-lee-cas

Do you have any brothers?

¿Tiene hermanos?
tye-ne er-mah-nos

Married?

¿Casados?
cah-sah-dos

With children?

¿Tienen hijos?
tye-nen ee-hos

Do you have any sisters?

¿Tiene hermanas?
tye-ne er-mah-nas

Married?

¿Casadas?
cah-sah-das

With children?

¿Tienen hijos?
tye-nen ee-hos

Is your father alive or dead?

¿Está su padre vivo o muerto?
es-tah soo pah-dreh vee-vo o mwer-to

How old is he?

¿Qué edad tiene?
ke eh-dad tye-neh

At what age did he die?

¿A qué edad murió?
ah ke eh-dad moo-ryo

Is he is good health?	¿Está en buena salud? es-tah en boo-eh-nah sah-looth
Is your mother dead or alive?	¿Está su madre viva o muerta? es-tah soo mah-dreh vee-vah o moo-er-ta
How old is she?	¿Qué edad tiene? ke eh-dad tye-ne
At what age did she die?	¿A qué edad murió? ah ke eh-dad moo-ryo
Is she in good health?	¿Está en buena salud? es-tah en boo-eh-nah sah-looth
Are there any illnesses that sure to run in the family? - For example, diabetes, tuberculosis or others.	¿Han habido enfermedades que han abundado en la familia? - por ejemplo, diabetes, tuberculosis u otras. an ah-bee-do en-fer-meh-dah-des ke an ah-boon-dah-do en la fah-mee-lya por e-hem-plo, dya-be-tes, too-ber-coo-lo-sis oo o-tras
Did you have mumps?	¿Tuvo papera o farfallota? too-vo pah-peh-rah o far-fah-lyo-tah
How old were you when you had the mumps?	¿Qué edad tenía cuando tuvo papera? ke eh-dad te-nya kwan-do too-vo peh-peh-rah
Did your testicles became swollen when you had mumps?	¿Se le incharon los testículos cuando tuvo papera? se le een-cha-ron los tes-tee-coo-los kwan-do too-vo pah-peh-rah
Have you had any serious illness?	¿Tuvo alguna enfermedad grave? too-vo al-goo-nah en-fer-meh-dad grah-veh
Have you had any operation?	¿Ha sido operado? ah see-do oh-peh-rah-do
Has your appendix been removed?	¿Le han sacado su apéndice? le ah sah-cah-do soo ah-pen-dee-se
Did you ever have an operation for a hernia?	¿Le han operado por alguna hernia o quebradura? le an oh-peh-rah-do por al-goo-nah er-nya o ke-brah-doo-rah

Did you ever have any operations near the testicles?

¿Ha tenido operaciones cerca de los testículos?
ah teh-nee-do oh-peh-rah-syo-nes cerka de los tes-tee-coo-los

Did you have any military service?

¿Ha estado en el servicio militar?
ah es-tah-do en el ser-vee-syo mee-lee-tar

Were you rejected from military service because of your health?

¿Ha sido rechazado para servicio militar debido a su salud?
ah see-do reh-chah-sah-do pah-rah ser-vee-syo mee-lee-tar de-bee-do ah soo sah-looth

Do you have any allergies?

¿Tiene alergias?
tye-ne ah-ler-hee-as

To what are you allergic?

¿A qué es usted alérgico?
ah ke es oos-teth ah-ler-hee-co

Do you take any medicines?

¿Está tomando medicinas?
es-tah to-man-do meh-dee-see-nas

Do you take vitamin pills?

¿Toma usted regularmente píldoras de vitaminas?
to-ma oos-teth reh-goo-lar-men-teh peel-do-ras de vee-tah-mee-nas

Do you usually take hot baths or do you usually take showers?

¿Toma usted regularmente baños calientes o regadera?
to-mah oos-teth reh-goo-lar-men-te bah-nyos ca-lyen-tes o reh-gah-deh-rah

Do you wear tight underpants which hold the testicles close to your body - "jockey shorts"?

¿Usa usted calzoncillos apretados que le sostienen los testículos contra el cuerpo, o sea suspensorios?
oo-sa oos-teth cal-son-see-lyos ah-pre-tah-dos ke le sos-tye-nen los tes-tee-coo-los con-trah el kwer-po, o se-ah soos-pen-so-ryos

Have you had any unusual exposure to x-rays?

¿Ha sido expuesto largamente a rayos x?
ah see-do ex-poo-es-to lar-gah-men-te ah rah-yos eh-kees

Have you ever had any type of treatment with x-rays - not just x-ray pictures?

¿Ha recibido algún tratamiento con rayos x?
ah reh-see-bee-do al-goon trah-tah-myen-to con ra-yos eh-kees

When you were an infant, were
both testicles in the scrotum or
did one or both testicles come
down into the scrotum later?

¿Cuando era infante tenía los testículos
en el escroto o uno o los dos testículos
descendieron mas tarde?
kwan-do eh-rah een-fan-teh teh-nya los
tes-tee-coo-los en el es-cro-to o oo-no
o los dos tes-tee-coo-los des-sen-dye-
ron mas tar-de

Did you receive injections to make
the testicles go into the scrotum?

¿Le dieron inyecciones para hacer bajar
los testículos dentro del escroto?
le dye-ron een-yek-syo-nes pah-rah ah-
ser bah-har los tes-tee-coo-los den-tro
del es-cro-to

Did you have an operation to make
the testicles go into the scrotum?

¿Fué operado para hacer bajar los testículos dentro del escroto?
foo-eh oh-peh-rah-do pah-ra ah-ser
bah-har los tes-tee-coo-los den-tro del
es-cro-to

Did you ever have any gonorrhea?

¿Tuvo gonorrea alguna vez?
too-vo go-no-rreh-ah al-goo-nah vez

How many times did you have
gonorrhea?

¿Cuántas veces tuvo gonorrea?
kwan-tas veh-ses too-vo go-no-rreh-ah

Did any doctor ever have to put any
instruments into your penis?

¿Algún doctor le ha puesto instrumentos
dentro de su pene?
al-goon dok-tor le ah pwes-to eens-troo-
men-tos den-tro de soo peh-neh

Did you ever have any operations
on the penis?

¿Ha tenido operaciones en el pene?
ah teh-nee-do oh-peh-rah-syo-nes en el
peh-neh

Did you ever have kidney stones?

¿Tuvo piedras en los riñones?
too-vo pee-eh-dras en los ree-nyo-nes

Did you ever have an operation to make
the testicles go into the scrotum?

¿Ha tenido alguna operación para hacer
que los testículos bajasen al escroto?
ah teh-nee-do al-goo-na o-peh-rah-syon
pah-rah ah-ser ke los tes-tee-coo-los
bah-ha-sen al es-cro-to

Did you ever have any swelling of
the testicles?

¿Tuvo alguna vez inchados los testículos?
too-vo al-goo-na ves een-chah-dos los
tes-tee-coo-los

Did a doctor ever tell you that you
have a hydrocele?

¿Le ha dicho algún doctor que usted
tiene un hidrocele?
le ah dee-cho al-goon dok-tor ke oos-
teh tye-ne oon ee-dro-seh-leh

Did a doctor ever tell you that you
have a varicocele?

¿Le ha dicho algún doctor que usted
tiene un varicocele?
le ah dee-cho al-goon dok-tor ke oos-
teh tye-ne oon vah-ree-co-seh-leh

Did you get any treatment to increase
the development of your sexual organs
when you were a child?

¿Recibió tratamiento para aumentar
el desarrollo de sus órganos genitales
cuando era niño?
reh-see-byo trah-tah-myen-to pah-rah
ah-oo-men-tar el deh-sah-rroh-yo de
soos or-gah-nos sek-soo-ah-les kwan-
do eh-rah nee-nyo

How often do you have sexual relation
with your wife?

¿Qué tan amenudo tiene relaciones
sexuales con su esposa?
ke tan ah-meh-noo-do tye-ne reh-lah-
syo-nes sek-soo-ah-les con soo es-po-
sah

Do you ejaculate each time you have
sexual relations?

¿Tiene ejaculación (se viene, o tiene
emisiones) cada vez que tiene relaciones
sexuales?
tye-ne eh-yah-coo-lah-syon (seh vye-ne
o tye-ne eh-mee-syo-nes) cah-dah vez
ke tye-ne reh-lah-syo-nes sek-soo-ah-
les

Do you practice coitus interruptus?

¿Practica relaciones sexuales inte-
rrumpidas (retira el pene al venirse)?
prak-tee-ka reh-lah-syo-nes sek-soo-
ah-les een-teh-room-pee-das (reh-tee-
rah el peh-neh al veh-neer-seh)

Do you have any pain when you
have sexual relations?

¿Siente usted dolor durante las relaciones sexuales?
syen-te oos-teth doh-lor doo-ran-te
las reh-lah-syo-nes sek-soo-ah-les

Have you ever had an examination
of the semen before?

¿Le han examinado el semen antes?
le an ek-sah-mee-nah-do el seh-men
an-tes

Were you told that the specimen was
weak?

¿Le han dicho que su muestra era
débil?
le an dee-cho ke soo moo-es-tra era
deh-beel

Were you given any treatments to
improve the semen?

¿Le han dado algunos tratamientos
para mejorar el semen?
le an dah-do al-goo-nos trah-tah-myen-
tos pah-rah meh-ho-rar el seh-men

Injections?

¿Inyecciones?
een-yek-syo-nes

Pills?

¿ Píldoras?
peel-do-ras

For how long did you get the
treatment?

¿ Por cuánto tiempo recibió el tratamiento?
por kwan-to tyem-po reh-see-byo el
trah-tah-myen-to

Did the specimen improve?

¿ Mejoró la muestra de semen?
meh-ho-ro la moo-es-tra de seh-men

QUESTIONS ON FEMALE INFERTILITY	PREGUNTAS SOBRE INFERTILIDAD DE LA MUJER pre-goon-tas so-bre een-fer-tee-lee- tha de lah moo-her
What is your name?	¿Cuál es su nombre? kwal es soo nom-bre
How old are you?	¿Qué edad tiene su esposo? ke eh-dad tye-ne soo es-po-so
Have you been previously married?	¿Ha sido casada antes? ah see-do cah-sah-da an-tes
Did you have any pregnancies by your previous husbands?	¿Ha tenido embarazos con sus otros maridos? ah teh-nee-do em-bah-rah-sos con soos o-tros mah-ree-dos
Have you had any pregnancies prior to your marriage?	¿Ha tenido embarazos antes de casarse? ah te-nee-do em-bah-rah-sos an-tes de cah-sar-seh
Has your present husband been married previously?	¿Ha estado su esposo casado antes de este matrimonio? ah es-ta-do soo es-po-so cah-sah-do an-tes de es-te mah-tree-mo-nyo
Did your present husband cause any pregnancies before this marriage?	¿Ha causado, su presente marido, embarazos antes de este matrimonio? ah cah-oo-sah-do, soo preh-sen-teh mah-ree-do, em-bah-rah-sos an-tes de es-te mah-tree-mo-nyo
Have there been any pregnancies in this marriage?	¿Ha tenido embarazos con este matri-monio? ah teh-nee-do em-bah-rah-sos con es-te mah-tree-mo-nyo
How many pregnancies have there been in this marriage?	¿Cuántos embarazos ha habido en este matrimonio? kwan-tos em-bah-rah-sos ah ah-bee-do en es-teh mah-tree-mo-nyo
Are you working also or are you just a housewife?	¿Trabaja usted tambien o es solamente ama de casa? trah-bah-ha oos-teth tam-byen o es so-lah-men-te ah-ma de cah-sa
What kind of work do you do?	¿Qué clase de trabajo hace? ke cla-seh de trah-ba-ho ah-se

What is your husban'd occupation?

¿Cuál es la ocupación de su marido?
kwal es la oh-coo-pah-syon de soo
mah-ree-do

What is your religion?

¿Cuál es su religión?
kwal es soo reh-lee-he-on

What is the religion of your husband?

¿Cuál es la religión de su marido?
kwal es la reh-lee-hee-on de soo mah-
ree-do

How long have you and your present
husband been married?

¿Qué tiempo tiene usted de casada con
su presente marido?
ke tyem-po tye-ne oos-teth de cah-sah-
da con soo pre-sen-te mah-ree-do

How many live children do you have?

¿Cuántas criaturas tiene vivas?
kwan-tas cree-ah-too-ras tye-ne vee-
vas

Were there any induced abortions?

¿Tuvo abortos provocados?
too-vo ah-bor-tos pro-vo-cah-dos

Were there any miscarriages?

¿Tuvo abortos espontáneos?
too-vo ah-bor-tos es-pon-tah-nyos

Did you have any ectopic (tubal)
pregnancies?

¿Tuvo algún embarazo fuera de la
matriz (ectópico) o en los tubos?
too-vo al-goon em-bah-rah-so foo-e-rah
de la mah-trees (ek-to-pee-co) o en los
too-bos

Did you have any babies born dead
(stillbirths)?

¿Ha tenido alguna criatura nacida
muerta?
ah teh-nee-do al-goo-nah cree-ah-too-
rah nah-see-dah moo-er-tah

In what years did you have pregnancies?

¿En qué años tuvo los embarazos?
en ke ah-nyos too-vo los em-bah-rah-
sos

If you became pregnant, did you
become pregnant quickly or did it
require a long time for you to become
pregnant?

¿Si usted se embarazó, fué enseguida,
o tardó mucho tiempo?
see oos-teth se em-bah-rah-so foo-eh
en-seh-gee-dah, o tar-doh moo-cho
tyem-po

Did you use any methods to prevent
pregnancies for a while after marriage?

¿Usó algún método para prevenir embarazos, temporalmente, después de
su casamiento?
oo-so al-goon meh-to-do pah-rah pre-
veh-neer em-bah-rah-sos, tem-po-ral-
men-teh, des-pwes de soo cah-sah-
myen-to

Did you use a diaphragm to prevent
pregnancies?

¿Usó diafragma para prevenir
embarazos?
oo-so dya-frag-mah pah-rah preh-veh-
neer em-bah-rah-sos

Douches?

¿Duchas?
doo-chas

Suppositories?

¿Supositorios?
soo-po-see-to-ryos

Foam?

¿Medicinas espumosas?
meh-dee-see-nas es-poo-mo-sas

Pills?

¿Pildoras?
peel-do-ras

Did your husband use condom (or
rubber)?

¿Usa su esposo condón?
oo-sa soo es-po-so con-don

Did your husband withdraw during sex
relations to prevent pregnancies?

¿Durante las relaciones sexuales se
retiró su esposo para evitar de dejar
el semen dentro de usted?
doo-ran-te las reh-lah-syo-nes sek-
soo-ah-les se reh-tee-ro soo es-po-so
pah-rah eh-vee-tar de deh-har el semen den-tro de oos-teth

For how long did you use measures to
avoid pregnancy?

¿Por cuánto tiempo usó medidas de
prevención de embarazo?
por kwan-to tyem-po oo-so meh-dee-das
de preh-ven-syon de em-bah-rah-so

Have you had any operation to prevent
more pregnancies?

¿Ha tenido alguna operación para prevenir más embarazos?
ah teh-nee-do al-goo-na o-peh-rah-syon
pah-rah preh-veh-neer mas em-bah-rah-
sos

Were your tubes tied or cut to
prevent pregnancy?

¿Fueron sus tubos atados, o cortados
para prevenir embarazos?
foo-eh-ron soos too-bos ah-tah-dos,
o cor-tah-dos pah-rah preh-veh-neer
em-bah-rah-sos

Were your tubes tied or removed
after your last pregnancy?

¿Fueron sus tubos atados o sacados
después de su último embarazo?
foo-eh-ron soos too-bos ah-tah-dos o
sah-cah-dos des-pwes de soo ool-tee-
mo em-bah-rah-so

Have you been in good general health?	¿Ha estado usted en buena salud en general? ah es-tah-do oos-teth en boo-eh-na sah-looth en geh-neh-ral
Is your weight steady?	¿Es su peso constante? es soo peh-so cons-tan-teh
Have you been gaining weight?	¿Está usted ganando peso? es-tah oos-teth gah-nan-do peh-so
Have you been losing weight?	¿Está usted perdiendo peso? es-tah oos-teth per-dyen-do peh-so
Do you sleep well?	¿Duerme bien? doo-er-meh byen
Is your appetite good?	¿Tiene buen apetito? tye-neh boo-en ah-peh-tee-to
Do you use tobacco? How much?	¿Usa tabaco? ¿Cuánto? oo-sah tah-bah-ko Kwan-to
Do you drink much alcoholic drinks?	¿Bebe muchas bebidas alcohólicas? beh-beh moo-chas beh-bee-das al-co o-lee-cas
Do you have any brothers?	¿Tiene hermanos? tye-ne er-mah-nos
Married?	¿Casados? cah-sah-dos
With children?	¿Tienen hijos? tye-nen ee-hos
Do you have any sisters?	¿Tiene hermanas? tye-ne er-mah-nas
Married?	¿Casadas? cah-sah-das
With children?	¿Tienen hijos? tye-nen ee-hos
Is your father alive or dead?	¿Está su padre vivo o muerto? es-tah soo pah-dreh vee-vo o moo-er-to
How old is he?	¿Qué edad tiene? ke eh-dad tye-neh
At what age did he die?	¿A qué edad murió? ah ke eh-dad moo-ryo

Is he in good health?	¿Está en buena salud? es-tah en boo-eh-nah sah-looth
Is your mother dead or alive?	¿Está su madre viva o muerta? es-tah soo mah-dreh vee-vah o moo-er-ta
How old is she?	¿Qué edad tiene? ke eh-dad tye-ne
At what age did she die?	¿A qué edad murió? ah ke eh-dad moo-ryo
Is she in good health?	¿Está en buena salud? es-tah en boo-eh-na sah-looth
Are there any illnesses that sure to run in the family? - For example, diabetes, tuberculosis or others.	¿Han habido enfermedades que han abundado en la familia? - por ejemplo, diabetes, tuberculosis u otras. an ah-bee-do en-fer-meh-dah-des ke an ah-boon-dah-do en la fah-mee-lya por e-hem-plo, dya-be-tes, too-ber-coo-lo-sees oo o-tras
Did you have any serious illnesses when you were a child?	¿Tuvo algunas enfermedades graves en la infancia? too-vo al-goo-nas en-fer-meh-dah-des grah-ves en lah een-fahn-cya
Did you have mumps?	¿Tuvo papera o farfallota? too-vo pah-peh-rah o far-fah-lyo-tah
At what age?	¿A qué edad? ah ke eh-dad
Did you get very sick with pain in the abdomen when you had mumps?	¿Tuvo dolores de vientre muy fuertes cuando la papera o farfallota? too-vo do-lo-res de vyen-treh moo-ee foo-er-tes kwan-do la pah-peh-rah o far-fah-lyo-tah
Have you had any serious illnesses as an adult?	¿Ha tenido algunas enfermedades graves desde que es adulto? ah teh-nee-do al-goo-nas en-fer-meh-dah-des grah-ves des-deh ke es ah-dool-to
Have you ever been in a hospital because of a sickness or operation?	¿Ha estado en algún hospital debido a enfermedad u operación? ah es-tah-do en al-goon os-pee-tal deh-bee-do ah en-fer-meh-dad oo o-peh-rah-syon

Do you have any allergies?

¿Tiene alergias?
tye-ne ah-ler-hee-as

    Allergic to penicillin?

¿Es alérgica a la penicilina?
es ah-ler-hee-cah ah la peh-nee-see-lee-nah

Are you allergic to any other
medicines?

¿Es alérgica a algunas otras medicinas?
es ah-ler-hee-ca ah al-goo-nas o-tras
meh-dee-see-nas

Do you take any medicines?

¿Está tomando algunas medicinas?
es-tah to-man-do al-goo-nas meh-dee-see-nas

What medicines do you take?

¿Qué medicinas toma?
ke meh-dee-see-nas to-mah

For what reason do you take medicines?

¿Cuál es la razón para tomar medicinas?
kwal es la rah-son pah-rah to-mar
meh-dee-see-nas

Do you take any medicines to regulate
your periods?

¿Toma algunas medicinas para regularizar sus periodos?
to-ma al-goo-nas meh-dee-see-nas pah-rah reh-goo-lah-ree-sar soos peh-ryo-dos

How old were you when you started
to menstruate?

¿A qué edad empezó usted a menstruar?
ah ke eh-dad em-peh-so oos-teth ah
mens-troo-ar

How many days are there from one
period of bleeding to the next?

¿Cuántos días entre cada periodo?
kwan-tos dy-as en-tre cah-dah peh-ryo-do

Is the interval between your periods
always regular?

¿Es el intervalo entre los periodos
siempre regular?
es el een-ter-vah-lo en-treh los peh-ryo-dos syem-pre re-goo-lar

How long does the blood flow last
during each period?

¿Cuánto tiempo le dura cada periodo?
kwan-to tyem-po le doo-rah cah-dah
peh-ryo-do

Is there a great deal, a small amount,
or moderate amount of bleeding?

¿Es mucha, o poca o moderada la cantidad de sangre?
es moo-cha, o po-ka, o mo-the-rah-dah la can-tee-dad de san-gre

When was your last period?

¿Cuándo fué su último periodo?
kwan-do foo-eh soo ool-tee-mo
peh-ryo-do

When was the period before that last one?

¿Cuándo fué el penúltimo periodo?
kwan-do foo-eh el pe-nool-tee-mo peh-ryo-do

Is your menstrual period overdue?

¿Está atrasada, al presente?
es-tah ah-trah-sah-tha al pre-sen-te

Did you have any pain during the bleeding?

¿Siente usted algún dolor durante la menstruación?
syen-teh oos-teth al-goon do-lor doo-ran-te la mens-troo-ah-syon

Before?

¿Antes?
ahn-tes

After?

¿Después?
des-pwes

Do you have any discharge other than blood from down below?

¿Tiene usted algún derrame o secreción además de sangre por sus partes privadas (o vagina)?
tye-ne oos-teth al-goon der-rah-meh, ah-de-mas de san-gre, por soos partes pree-va-thas (o va-hee-nah)

When was the last time you had intercourse?

¿Cuándo fué la última vez que tuvo relaciones sexuales?
kwan-do foo-eh la ool-tee-mah ves ke too-vo reh-lah-syo-nes sek-soo-ah-les

Do you think it is possible that you are now pregnant?

¿Cree usted que sea posible que esté en estado (o embarazada)?
creh oos-teth ke seh-ah po-see-bleh ke es-teh en es-tah-do (o em-bah-rah-sah-da)

What is the color of your menstrual blood?

¿Cuál es el color de su sangre?
kwal es el co-lor de soo san-greh

- Red

Roja
ro-ha

- Dark red

Roja oscura
ro-ha os-koo-rah

- Light red

Roja clara
ro-ha cla-rah

- Blood tinged

Rosada
ro-sah-tha

- Chocolate

Chocolate
cho-ko-lah-teth

Do you pass large blood clots?	¿Pasa usted coágulos de sangre muy grandes? pah-sah oos-teth co-ah-goo-los de sangreh moo-ee gran-des
Did you have a miscarriage? (An abortion?)	¿Tuvo aborto accidental o provocado? too-vo ah-bor-to ak-see-den-tal o pro-vo-ka-tho
Do you get pain in the abdomen each month about half way between your periods?	¿Le dan dolores de vientre cada mes a la mitad entre los periodos? le dan do-lo-res de vyen-tre cah-dah mes a la mee-tad en-treh los peh-ryo-dos
Do you get vaginal staining between your periods?	¿Tiene manchas de sangre en el intervalo entre los periodos? tye-ne man-chas de san-greh en el eenter-vah-lo en-treh los peh-ryo-dos
Do you have any vaginal discharge between your periods?	¿Tiene alguna descarga vaginal entre los periodos? tye-ne al-goo-na des-car-ga vah-heenal en-tre los peh-ryo-dos
Do your breasts get swollen or tender before your periods?	¿Se le hinchan los senos o se le ponen adoloridos antes de sus periodos? se le een-chan los seh-nos o seh le po-nen ah-do-lo-ree-dos an-tes de soos peh-ree-oh-dos
Do you get very irritable before your periods (pre-menstrual tension)?	¿Se vuelve irritable antes de los periodos (tensión premenstrual)? se voo-el-veh ee-ree-tah-ble an-tes de los peh-ryo-dos (ten-syon pre-menstroo-al
Do you have pains before your periods?	¿Le dan dolores antes de sus periodos? le dan do-lo-res an-tes de soos peh-ryo-dos
How often do you and your husband have sexual relations?	¿Qué tan amenudo usted y su esposo tienen relaciones sexuales? ke tan ah-meh-noo-do oos-teth ee soo es-poh-so tye-nen reh-lah-syo-nes sek-soo-ah-les
Do you have more desire to have sexual relations than your husband?	¿Tiene usted mas deseo de tener relaciones sexuales que su esposo? tye-ne oos-teth mas deh-seh-o de tehner reh-la-syo-nes sek-soo-ah-les ke soo es-po-so

Does your husband has more desire
to have sexual relations than you do?

¿Tiene su marido mas deseo de tener
relaciones sexuales que usted?
tye-ne soo mah-ree-do mas deh-seh-oh
de teh-ner reh-lah-syo-nes sek-soo-ah-
les ke oos-teth

Do you have pain during sexual
relations?

¿Siente dolor durante sus relaciones
sexuales?
syen-te do-lor doo-ran-te soos reh-lah-
syo-nes sek-soo-ah-les

Is the pain in the vagina?

¿Es el dolor vaginal?
es el do-lor vah-hee-nal

Is the pain in the abdomen?

¿Es el dolor en el vientre?
es el do-lor en el vyen-tre

Do you reach a climax (orgasm) during
sexual relations?

¿Llega a tener una sensación de gran
placer (orgasmo o clímax) durante el
contacto?
lye-gah ah teh-ner oo-na sen-sah-syon
de gran plah-cer (or-gas-mo o clee-
max) doo-ran-teh el con-tak-to

Do you remain in bed after sexual
relations?

¿Se queda en la cama después del contacto sexual?
se keh-dah en la cah-mah des-pwes del
con-tak-to sek-soo-al

Do you douche immediately after
sexual relations?

¿Se da duchas después de las relaciones sexuales?
se dah doo-chas des-pwes de las reh-
lah-syo-nes sek-soo-ah-les

Do you go to the bathroom to urinate
immediately after sexual relations?

¿Va usted al cuarto de baño a orinar
inmediatamente después del contacto
sexual?
vah oos-teth al kwar-to de bah-nyo ah
o-ree-nar een-meh-dya-tah-men-te
des-pwes del con-tak-to sek-soo-al

When you have sexual relations is your
husband able to insert his penis deeply
into the vagina?

¿Cuando usted tiene relaciones sexuales, puede su marido penetrar el pene
muy profundamente dentro de la vagina?
kwan-do oos-teth tye-ne reh-lah-syo-
nes sek-soo-ah-les, pwe-de soo mah-
ree-do peh-neh-trar el peh-neh moo-ee
pro-foon-dah-men-te den-tro de la
vah-hee-na

Does your husband get strong erections?	¿ Tiene su marido erecciones fuertes? tye-ne soo mah-ree-do eh-rek-syo-nes foo-er-tes
Have you had any previous treatment to help you have a baby?	¿ Ha tenido usted algún tratamiento anteriormente para ayudarle a tener una criatura? ah teh-nee-do oos-teth al-goon trah-tah-myen-to an-teh-ryor-men-te pah-rah ah-yoo-dar-le ah teh-ner oo-nah cree-ah-too-rah
Has your husband had previous treatment to help him to have a baby?	¿ Ha sido su esposo tratado anterior-mente para ayudarlo a tener una cria-tura? ah see-do soo es-po-so trah-tah-do an-teh-ryor-men-te pah-rah ah-yoo-dar-lo ah teh-ner oo-na cree-ah-too-ra
What is the name and address of the doctor that treated you or your husband previously?	¿ Cuál es el nombre y la dirección del doctor que trató anteriormente a usted o a su esposo? kwal es el nom-bre ee la dee-rec-syon del dok-tor ke trah-to an-teh-ryor-men-te ah oos-teth o ah soo es-po-so
The doctor's telephone number?	¿ El número de teléfono del doctor? el noo-meh-ro deh teh-leh-fo-no del dok-tor
It was a pleasure to consult you	Fué un placer consultarle foo-eh oon pla-ser con-sool-tar-leh
The next visit will be on:	La próxima visita será en: lah prox-ee-ma vee-see-ta seh-rah en:
month:	mes: mehs
day:	día: dee-ah
hour:	hora: oh-rah

THE PROCTOLOGIC EXAMINATION

EL EXAMEN PROCTOLOGICO
el ek-sah-men prok-toh-loh-hee-co

Sit down, please

Sientese, por favor.
syen-teh-seh, por fah-vor

What is your full name?

¿Cuál es su nombre completo?
kwal es soo nom-breh com-pleh-to

What is your address?

¿Cuál es su dirección?
kwal es soo dee-rek-syon

Your telephone number?

¿Su teléfono?
soo teh-leh-foh-no

What is your occupation?

¿Cuál es su ocupación?
kwal es soo o-coo-pah-syon

How old are you?

¿Qué edad tiene?
ke eh-dad tye-ne

Where were you born?

¿Dónde nació?
don-deh nah-syo

What is troubling you?

¿Qué le molesta?
ke leh mo-les-tah

Are you loosing weight?

¿Está perdiendo peso?
es-tah per-dyen-do peh-so

Are you weak?

¿Se siente débil?
se syen-te deh-beel

Do you suffer from constipation or
diarrhea?

¿Sufre usted de estreñimiento o
diarrea?
soo-freh oos-teth de es-treh-nee-
myen-to o dyah-reh-ah

Did you have any kind of rectal or
intestinal trouble in the past?

¿Tuvo usted alguna enfermedad del
ano o el intestino?
too-vo oos-teh al-goo-nah en-fer-meh-
dad del ah-no o el een-tes-tee-no

Did you ever have blood in the stools?
Very dark? Bright red?

¿Tuvo alguna vez sangre en su excre-
mento? ¿Muy obscuro? ¿Muy rojo?
too-vo al-goo-na ves san-gre en soo
ex-creh-men-to moo-ee obs-coo-roh
moo-ee ro-ho

Do you bleed easily on the slightest
injury?

¿Sangra usted facilmente a la menor
herida?
san-grah oos-teth fah-seel-men-te ah
la meh-nor eh-ree-da

Have you had:	¿Ha tenido usted: ah teh-nee-do oos-teth
Gonorrhea?	¿Gonorrea? goh-no-reh-ah
Syphilis?	¿Sífilis? see-fee-lees
Chancre?	¿Chancro? chan-cro
Inguinal swollen glands?	¿Glándulas hinchadas en las ingles? glan-doo-las een-chah-das en las een-gles
Tuberculosis?	¿Tuberculosis? too-ber-coo-lo-sees
Some other diseases of the anus?	¿Algunas otras enfermedades del ano? al-goo-nas o-tras en-fer-meh-dah-des del ah-no
Do you have trouble with the rectum or moving your bowels?	¿Tiene usted dificultades al obrar? tye-ne oos-teth dee-fee-cool-tah-des al o-brar
Do you bleed when your bowels move?	¿Sangra cuando obra? san-grah kwan-do o-brah
Spots of blood only?	¿Manchas de sangre solamente? man-chas de san-greh so-lah-men-teh
Free bleeding?	¿Sangre en abundancia? san-greh en ah-boon-dan-sya
Do you have pain during the bowel action?	¿Siente usted dolor durante la evacua- ción? syen-te oos-teth do-lor doo-ran-teh la eh-vah-coo-ah-syon
Is the pain continuous or intermittent?	¿Es el dolor continuo o intermitente? es el do-lor con-tee-noo-oh oh een- ter-mee-ten-teh
Is there pain after defecation and how long does it last?	¿Tiene dolor después de defecar y cuánto le dura? tye-ne do-lor des-pwes de deh-feh-car ee cwan-to leh doo-rah

Is there a swelling or a lump at the
arms?

¿Tiene hinchazón o un bulto en el ano?
tye-ne een-chah-son o oon bool-to en
el ah-no

Is it painful?   How long has it been
there?

¿Es doloroso?   ¿Cuánto tiempo lo ha
tenido?
es do-lo-ro-so   kwan-to tyem-po lo
ah teh-nee-do

Is there a purulent or mucus discharge
from the swelling?

¿Tiene supuración o secreción en la
hinchazón?
tye-neh soo-poo-rah-syon o seh-creh-
syon en la een-chah-son

When the bowels move does the rectum
came out (prolapse)?

¿Cuando obra se le sale el recto
(prolapso)?
kwan-do oh-brah se le sah-leh el rek-
to (pro-lap-sah)

Does it return by itself (spontaneously)
or is manual replacement necessary?

¿Se vuelve a su sitio por si solo
(espontaneamente) o lo tiene que hacer
manualmente?
se voo-el-veh ah soo see-tee-o por see
so-lo (es-pon-tah-neh-ah-men-te) oh
lo tye-neh ke ah-ser mah-noo-al-men-
teh

Does itching or burning occur at
the anus?

¿Le pica o le quema el recto?
le pee-ka o le keh-mah el rek-to

Is this worse before or after a bowel
movement?

¿Es peor antes o después de obrar?
es peh-or an-tes o des-pwes de o-brar

Is itching severe after retiring?

¿La comezón es peor al acostarse?
la co-meh-son es peh-or al ah-cos-
tar-seh

Does it wake you at night?

¿Lo despierta durante la noche?
lo des-pyer-tah doo-ran-teh la no-cheh

Do you eat spicy food?

¿Come usted comidas picantes?
coh-meh oos-teth co-mee-das pee-kan-
tes

Is there a history of hemorrhoids or
rectal tumors in your family?

¿Han habido casos de almorranas o
tumores del recto entre sus familia-
res?
an ah-bee-do cah-sos de al-moh-rrah-
nas o too-mo-res del rek-to en-treh
soos fah-mee-lya-res

Do you take enemas?

¿Usa enemas (o lavativas)?
oo-sah eh-neh-mas (o lah-vah-tee-vas)

Do you take laxatives?	¿Toma usted purgantes? to-mah oos-teth poor-gan-tes
What laxatives do you take?	¿Qué purgantes toma? ke poor-gan-tes to-mah
Milk of magnesia?	¿Leche de magnesia? leh-cheh de mag-neh-sya
Mineral oil?	¿Aceite mineral? ah-seh-ee-teh mee-neh-ral
Magnesia and Oil (M-O)?	¿Magnesia y Aceite? mag-neh-sya ee ah-seh-ee-teh
Ex-Lax?	¿Ex-Lax? ex - lax
Alophen pills?	¿Píldoras de alofen? peel-do-ras de ah-lo-fen
Coroid and bile salts tablets?	¿Tabletas de "Caroid and bile salts"? tah-bleh-tas deh "Caroid and bile salts?
Any other laxative?	¿Algún otro purgativo? al-goon oh-tro poor-gah-tee-vo
Do you use suppositories?	¿Usa supositorios? oo-sah soo-po-see-to-ryos
Of glycerine?	¿De glicerina? de glee-seh-ree-nah
Do you use medicated suppositories for your hemorrhoids?	¿Usa usted supositorios medicados para sus almorranas? oo-sah oos-teth soo-po-see-to-ryos meh-dee-cah-dos pah-rah soos al- moh-rah-nas
Please undress completely	Por favor, desvístase completamente por fah-vor, des-vees-tah-seh com- pleh-tah-men-te
Remove your:	Quítese: kee-teh-seh
- pants	- los pantalones los pan-tah-lo-nes
- panties	- la pantaloneta la pan-tah-lo-neh-tah

- shoes

- los zapatos
los sah-pah-tos

- coat

- el saco
el sah-co

- dress

- el vestido
el ves-tee-do

Get on the table

Subase sobre la mesa
soo-bah-seh so-breh la meh-sah

Lay down

Acuestese
ah-kwes-teh-seh

Turn over the right side

Acuestese sobre el lado derecho
ah-kwes-teh-seh so-breh el lah-do
deh-reh-cho

Turn over the left side

Acuestese sobre el lado izquierdo
ah-kwes-teh-seh so-breh el lah-do
ees-kyer-do

Turn face down

Volteese boca abajo
vol-teh-eh-seh bo-cah ah-bah-ho

Turn face up

Volteese boca arriba
vol-teh-eh-seh bo-cah ah-ree-bah

Kneel down and bring the chest
against the table

Arrodillase y ponga el pecho sobre
la mesa
ah-rro-dee-yah-seh ee pon-gah el
peh-cho so-breh lah meh-sah

Please flex your right thigh over the
abdomen with the knee flexed

Por favor doble su muslo derecho
sobre el vientre con la rodilla flexio-
nada.
por fah-vor do-bleh soo moos-lo deh-
reh-cho so-breh el vyen-treh con la
ro-dee-ya flex-syo-nah-dah

Flex your left thigh over the abdomen
with the knee flexed

Doble su muslo izquierdo sobre el
vientre con la rodilla doblada.
do-bleh soo moos-lo ees-kyer-do
so-breh el vyen-treh con la ro-dee-ya
do-blah-dah

Bear down as if you were to move
the bowels

Puje como si fuese a obrar.
poo-he co-mo see foo-eh-seh ah
oh-brar

I am going to introduce an instrument into the rectum to examine it	Le voy a introducir un instrumento en el recto para examinarlo. leh vo-ee ah een-tro-doo-seer oon een-troo-men-to en el rek-to pah-rah ex-sah-mee-nar-lo
It is going to bother you only slightly - relax	Le va a molestar un poco solamente - tranquilicese. le vah ah mo-les-tar oon po-co so-lah-men-teh - tran-kee-lee-seh-seh
Bear down	Puje poo-heh
Breathe with your mouth open	Respire con la boca abierta res-pee-reh con la bo-cah ah-byer-tah
Do not move	No se mueva no seh moo-eh-vah
I have finished	He terminado eh ter-mee-nah-do
Get dressed	Vístase vees-tah-seh
Treatment:	Tratamiento: trah-tah-myen-to
You need an operation	Usted necesita una operación oos-teh neh-seh-see-tah oo-nah o-peh-rah-syon
You need medicine	Usted necesita medicina oos-teh neh-seh-see-tah meh-dee-see-nah
I want you to take this medicine	Quiero que tome esta medicina kye-ro ke to-meh es-tah meh-dee-see-nah
Take one pill once a day	Tome una píldora una vez por día to-meh oo-nah peel-do-rah oo-nah ves por dee-ah
Take two tablets 2 times a day	Tome dos pastillas dos veces al día to-meh dos pas-tee-yas dos veh-ses al dee-ah
- before meals	- antes de las comidas an-tes de las co-mee-das
- after meals	- después de las comidas des-pwes de las co-mee-das

- before going to bed	- antes de acostarse an-tes de ah-cos-tar-seh
- when you wake up in the morning	- al levantarse por la mañana al leh-van-tar-seh por la mah-nya-nah
Take sitz baths:	Tome baños de asiento to-meh ba-nyos de ah-syen-to
- once a day	- una vez por día oo-nah ves por dee-ah
- twice a day	- dos veces por día dos veh-ses por dee-ah
- three times a day	- tres veces por día tres veh-ses por dee-ah
- every 4 hours	- cada cuatro horas cah-dah kwa-tro oh-ras
Take the sitz bath for:	Tome los baños de asiento por: to-meh los bah-nyos deh ah-syen-to por:
- 15 minutes	- 15 minutos 15 mee-noo-tos
- 30 minutes	- 30 minutos 30 mee-noo-tos
- 45 minutes	- 45 minutos 45 mee-noo-tos
- 1 hour	- 1 hora 1 o-rah
You have:	Usted tiene: oos-teh tye-neh
- an irritation	- irritación ee-ree-tah-syon
- an inflammation	- inflamación een-flah-mah-syon
- an eruption	- erupción eh-roop-syon
- ulcerations or ulceration	- ulceraciones o ulceración ool-seh-rah-syo-nes o ool-seh-rah-syon
- a fissures or fissures	- grietas o partidura gree-eh-tas o par-tee-doo-rah

- a fistula or fistulas

- tightness of the anus

- hemorrhoids

- a polyp or polyps

- a tumor

- a venereal disease

- tuberculosis

- anal tabs

- an abscess

- parasites

- a foreign body

- a traumatized rectum

- a prolapsed rectum

You are bleeding

Stop working until ..

Are you insured?

- fístula o fístulas
fees-too-lah o fees-too-las

- estrechez del ano
es-treh-ches del ah-no

- almorranas
al-mo-rah-nas

- pólipo o pólipos
poh-lee-po o poh-lee-pos

- tumor
too-mor

- enfermedad venérea
en-fer-meh-dah veh-neh-re-ah

- tuberculosis
too-ber-coo-lo-sees

- lengüetas o apendices de piel alrededor del ano
len-goo-eh-tas o ah-pen-dee-ses de
pyel al-reh-deh-dor del ah-no

- absceso (o apostema)
abs-seh-so (o ah-pos-teh-mah)

- parásitos
pah-rah-see-tos

- un objecto extraño
oon ob-heh-to ex-trah-nyo

- herido o traumatizado el recto
eh-ree-do o trah-oo-mah-tee-sah-do
el rek-to

- prolapso del recto
pro-lap-so del rek-to

Usted está sangrando
oos-teh es-tah san-gran-do

Deje de trabajar hasta ...
Deh-heh deh trah-bah-har as-tah

¿Está asegurado?
es-tah ah-seh-goo-rah-do

Is your insurance covering hospitali-
zation, medical and surgical expenses?

¿Cubre su seguro los gastos de hospital, visitas médicas y cirugía?
coo-breh soo seh-goo-ro los gas-tos
de os-pee-tal, vee-see-tas meh-dee-cas
ee see-roo-hee-ah

Does your insurance pay the
doctor's fee?

¿Paga su seguro la cuenta del doctor?
pah-gah soo seh-goo-ro la kwen-tah del
dok-tor

You owe me:

$ ....

Usted me debe:
oos-teh meh deh-beh:
$ ....

Return to work on :

Vuelva a trabajar en:
voo-el-vah ah trah-bah-har en:

Your case is finished

Su caso está terminado
soo cah-so es-tah ter-mee-nah-do

Return on:

Vuelva:
voo-el-vah

..... days

..... días
dee-as

..... weeks

..... semanas
seh-mah-nas

..... months

..... meses
meh-ses

It was a pleasure treating you

Fué un placer el tratarlo
foo-eh oon plah-ser el trah-tar-lo

88

ANESTHESIOLOGY

Good morning

Good afternoon

Good evening

Is your name:

Mr., Mrs., Miss, ...

What is your doctor's name?

I am Dr. .... from the
department of anesthesia

I am going to give you the anesthesia
tomorrow.

in the morning

in the afternoon

An associate of mine is going to
give you your anesthetic

After the operation you will be taken
into the Recovery Room

ANESTESIOLOGIA
ah-nes-teh-syo-lo-hee-ah

Buenos días
bwe-nos dyas

Buenas tardes
bwe-nas tar-des

Buenas noches
bwe-nas no-ches

¿Es su nombre:
es soo nom-breh

Señor, señora, señorita ....
seh-nyor, seh-nyo-rah, seh-nyo-ree-tah

¿Cuál es el nombre de su doctor?
kwal es el nom-breh de soo dok-tor

Yo soy el Dr. .... del departamento
de anestesia
yo soy el Dr. .... del deh-par-tah-
men-to de ah-nes-teh-sya

Yo le daré la anestesia mañana.
yo le dah-reh la ah-nes-teh-sya mah-
nyah-nah

por la mañana
por la mah-nyah-na

por la tarde
por la tar-deh

Algún asociado mío le va a dar el
anestético
al-goon ah-so-sya-do myo le vah ah
dar el ah-nes-teh-tee-co

Después de la operación usted será
llevada a la Sala de Recuperación.
des-pwes de lah o-peh-ra-syon oos-teth
seh-rah lleh-vah-dah ah la sah-lah deh
reh-coo-peh-rah-syon

You will remain in the Recovery Room until fully reckecked and your condition found good	Usted permanecerá en la Sala de Recuperación hasta que se le examine y su condición esté buena oos-teth per-mah-neh-seh-rah en la sah-la de reh-coo-peh-rah-syon as-tah keh seh le ex-sah-mee-neh ee soo con-dee-syon es-teh bwe-nah
After that you will be taken back to your room	Después de esto será llevada a su cuarto des-pwes de es-to seh-rah lleh-vah-dah ah soo kwar-to
I am going to ask you some pertinent questions	Le voy a preguntar algunas cosas muy pertinentes le vo-ee ah preh-goon-tar al-goo-nas co-sas mooy per-tee-nen-tes
It is important to recheck the questions although they are in the record	Es importante verificar las preguntas aunque ya están en su registro es eem-por-tan-teh veh-ree-fee-car las preh-goon-tas ah-oon-ke yah es-tan en soo reh-hees-tro
Do you have?:	¿Tiene usted? tye-ne oos-teth
Allergies?	alergias ah-ler-hee-as
to what?	¿A qué? ah ke
Are you taking medicines at home?	¿Está tomando medicinas en su casa? es-tah to-man-do meh-dee-cee-nas en soo cah-sah
What medicines are they?	¿Qué medicinas toma? ke meh-dee-see-nas to-mah
For what conditions do you take them?	¿Por qué causa las toma? por ke cah-oo-sah las to-mah
Do you take them for:	¿Las toma para: las to-mah pah-rah
the heart	el corazón el co-rah-son
the kidneys	los riñones los ree-nyo-nes
the lungs	los pulmones los pool-mo-nes

high blood pressure	la presión alta de sangre lah preh-syon al-tah deh san-greh
low blood pressure	la presión baja de sangre lah preh-syon bah-ha deh san-greh
What are the names of the medicines you are taking?	¿Cuáles son los nombres de las medicinas que usted toma? kwa-les son los nom-bres de las meh-dee-see-nas keh oos-teth to-mah
How long have you been taking them?	¿Cuánto tiempo hace que las toma? kwan-to tyem-po ah-se keh las to-mah
Who prescribed them, your surgeon or your medical man?	¿Quién se las recetó, su cirujano o su médico? kyen se las reh-seh-to, soo see-roo-hah-no o soo meh-dee-co
What kind of operation are you going to have?	¿Qué clase de operación va a tener? keh clah-seh de o-peh-rah-syon vah ah teh-ner
Were you operated before?	¿Ha sido operado (a) (fem.) antes? ah see-do oh-peh-rah-do (da) an-tes
What kind of operations did you have?	¿Qué clase de operaciones tuvo usted? keh clah-seh de oh-peh-rah-syo-nes too-vo oos-teth
Did you have any trouble with the anesthesia?	¿Tuvo algún trastorno con la anestesia? too-vo al-goon tras-tor-no con la ah-nes-teh-sya
What kind of trouble?	¿Qué clase de trastorno? keh clah-seh de tras-tor-no
What kind of anesthesia did you have?	¿Qué clase de anestesia tuvo usted? keh clah-seh de ah-nes-teh-sya too-vo oos-teth
You are going to have the anesthesia given through the back with a needle	Usted va a tener la anestesia por la cintura con una aguja oos-teh vah ah teh-ner la ah-nes-teh-sya por la seen-too-rah con oo-nah ah-goo-ha
You are going to go to sleep with an injection in the arm - then you will have the anesthesia by breathing	Va a dormir con anestesia inyectada en el brazo - y después va a respirar el anestético vah ah dor-meer con ah-nes-teh-sya een-yek-tah-dah en el brah-so - ee des-pwes vah ah res-pee-rar el ah-nes-teh-tee-co

I am going to inject the anesthesia
around the site of the operation

Voy a inyectar la anestesia alrededor
del sitio de la operación
voy ah een-yek-tar la ah-nes-teh-sya
al-reh-deh-dor del see-tee-oh de la
oh-peh-rah-syon

Do not worry - all know their work
around here - relax

No se apure - todos conocen lo que
hacen aquí - tranquilícese.
no se ah-poo-reh - to-dos co-no-sen
lo keh ah-sen ah-kee - tran-kee-lee-seh-
seh

A doctor cannot guarantee anything.
We all do the best we can

El doctor no puede garantizar nada.
Todos nosotros hacemos lo mejor que
podemos.
el dok-tor no pwe-deh gah-ran-tee-sar
nah-dah. to-dos no-so-tros ah-seh-
mos lo meh-hor keh po-deh-mos

Get on the operating table

Cambie sobre la mesa de operaciones
cam-bee-eh so-bre la meh-sah de
oh-peh-rah-syo-nes

Lay down on your back

Acuéstese sobre la espalda
ah-kwes-teh-seh so-breh la es-pal-dah

Lay down on your stomach

Acuéstese sobre el estómago
ah-kwes-teh-se so-breh el es-to-mah-
go

Lay over the right side

Acuéstese sobre el lado derecho
ah-kwes-teh-seh so-breh el lah-do
deh-reh-cho

Lay over the left side

Acuéstese sobre el lado izquierdo
ah-kwes-teh-seh so-breh el lah-do
ees-kee-ehr-do

Sit up on the table

Siéntese en la mesa
syen-teh-seh en la meh-sah

Sit up with legs hanging on the side
of the table

Siéntese con las piernas colgando sobre
el lado de la mesa
syen-teh-seh con las pyer-nas col-gan-
do so-breh el lah-do de la meh-sah

Breathe normally

Respire normalmente
res-pee-reh nor-mal-men-teh

Hold your breath

Sostenga la respiración
sos-ten-gah la res-pee-rah-syon

Bend your head forward	Doble su cabeza sobre el pecho do-bleh soo cah-beh-sah so-breh el peh-cho
Bend your head backward	Doble su cabeza para atrás do-bleh soo cah-beh-sah pah-rah ah-tras
Cough	Tosa to-sah
Breathe with the mouth open	Respire con la boca abierta res-pee-reh con la bo-cah ah-byer-tah
Expectorate (or spit)	Expectore (o escupa) ex-pek-to-reh (o es-coo-pah)
Move over to the stretcher	Muévase sobre la camilla moo-eh-vah-seh so-breh la cah-mee-lya
Yesterday you took the anesthesia very well	Ayer usted tomó la anestesia muy bien ah-ee-ehr oos-teth to-mo la ah-nes-teh-sya moo-ee byen
Do you have insurance to cover the anesthesia fee?	¿Tiene seguro para cubrir el precio de la anestesia? tye-neh seh-goo-ro pah-rah coo-breer el preh-syo de la ah-nes-teh-sya
Give me the blanks to fill out	Deme las planillas para llenarlas deh-meh las plah-nee-lyas pah-rah lye-nar-las
If you have no insurance you will receive from me a bill	Si usted no tiene seguro recibirá un recibo mio see oos-teh no tye-neh seh-goo-ro reh-see-bee-rah oon reh-see-bo myo
What is the name of your insurance?	¿Cuál es el nombre de su seguro? kwal es el nom-breh de soo seh-goo-ro
What is the number of your policy?	¿Cuál es el número de su póliza? kwal es el noo-meh-ro de soo po-lee-sah
Very glad to have served you	Muy contento de haberle servido moo-ee con-ten-to de ah-ber-leh ser-vee-do

PRESENT LABOR HISTORY

HISTORIA DEL PARTO PRESENTE
ees-to-rya del par-to preh-sen-teh

At what time did the labor pains
started?

¿A qué hora principiaron los dolores
de parto?
ah keh oh-rah preen-see-pee-ah-ron
los do-lo-res de par-to

At the start how often did the pains
come?

¿Al principio, que tan a menudo tenía
los dolores?
al preen-see-pyo keh tan ah meh-noo-
do teh-nya los do-lo-res

How often are the pains coming now?

¿Que tan a menudo le ocurren los dolores ahora?
keh tan ah meh-noo-do le o-koo-rren
los do-lo-res a-oh-rah

Are they real pains or just a back-
ache?

¿Son dolores verdaderos de parto o
solamente dolores de espalda?
son do-lo-res ver-dah-deh-ros de par-
to o so-lah-men-teh do-lo-res de es-
pal-dah

At the start how long did each pain
last?

¿Al principio cuánto tiempo duró cada
dolor?
al preen-see-pyo kwan-to tyem-po doo-
ro kah-dah do-lor

How long does each pain last now?

¿Cuánto tiempo dura ahora cada dolor?
kwan-to tyem-po doo-rah ah-oh-rah
kah-dah do-lor

Did the labor pains stop completely
for any length of time?

¿Se le pararon los dolores de parto
completamente por algún tiempo?
seh leh pah-rah-ron los do-lo-res de
par-to com-pleh-tah-men-teh por al-
goon tyem-po

When?

¿Cuándo?
kwan-do

For how long did they stop before
starting again?

¿Cuánto tiempo pasó antes de empezar-
de nuevo?
kwan-to tyem-po pah-so an-tes de em-
peh-sar deh noo-eh-vo

Did the bag of water break?

¿Se le rompió la bolsa de agua?
seh leh rom-pyo la bol-sah deh ah-
goo-ah

When?

¿Cuándo?
kwan-do

Did a lot of warm water rush out of
your vagina?

Salió precipitadamente mucha agua
caliente de su vagina?
sah-lyo preh-see-pee-tah-dah-men-teh
moo-chah ah-goo-ah cah-lyen-teh de
soo vah-he-nah

When did you eat last?

¿Cuándo fué su última comida?
kwan-do foo-eh soo ool-tee-mah co-
mee-dah

AT THE DELIVERY ROOM	EN LA SALA DE ALUMBRAMIENTO ehn la sah-lah de ah-loom-brah-myen-to
Please remove your artificial teeth	Por favor remueva su dentadura. por fah-vor reh-moo-eh-vah soo den-tah-doo-rah
Please remove your rings	Por favor quítese los anillos. por fah-vor kee-teh-seh los ah-nee-lyos
You must help us. Push	Usted debe ayudarnos, puje. oos-teh deh-beh ah-yoo-dar-nos, poo-heh
Breath in and out	Respire adentro y afuera res-pee-reh ah-den-tro ee ah-foo-eh-rah
Please breathe normally	Por favor, respire normalmente. por fah-vor, res-pee-reh nor-mal-men-teh
This injection will relieve your pain	Esta inyección le aliviará el dolor es-tah een-yek-syon le ah-lee-vee-ah-rah el do-lor
The baby will be born in ...... hours	La criatura nacerá en .... horas. lah cree-ah-too-rah nah-seh-rah en .... oh-ras
The baby will be born very soon	La criatura nacerá muy pronto la cree-ah-too-rah nah-seh-rah moo-ee pron-to
Where is your husband?	¿Dónde está su esposo? don-deh es-tah soo es-po-so
Your wife will need a Caesarean operation	Su señora necesitará una operación cesárea soo seh-nyo-rah neh-seh-see-tah-rah oo-nah o-peh-rah-syon seh-sah-reh-ah
Her labor is too slow	El parto de ella es muy lento el par-to deh eh-ya es moo-ee len-to
her pelvis is too small for the baby to be born without a caesarean operation	Su pelvis es demasiado pequeña para que la criatura pueda nacer sin una operación cesárea soo pel-vees es deh-mah-sya-do peh-keh-nya pah-rah keh la cree-ah-too-rah pwe-dah nah-ser seen oo-nah o-peh-rah-syon seh-sah-reh-ah

It is better for the baby

Es mejor para la criatura
es meh-hor pah-rah la cree-ah-too-rah

Will you please sign your permission
here

Por favor firme su permiso aquí
por fah-vor feer-meh soo per-mee-soh
ah-kee

| AFTER THE DELIVERY | DESPUES DEL PARTO |
| | des-pwes del par-to |

It is a fine baby

Es un hermoso niño
es oon ehr-mo-so nee-nyo

It is a fine girl

Es una hermosa niña
es oo-nah ehr-mo-sah nee-nya

The baby was not born alive

La criatura no nació viva
la cree-ah-too-rah no nah-syo vee-vah

I have to put a few stitches into your vagina so that you will be just as good as new

Voy a darle unas puntadas en la vagina
y así se sentirá usted como nueva
voy ah dar-leh oo-nas poon-tah-das
en la vah-hee-nah ee ah-see seh sen-
tee-rah oos-teth co-mo noo-eh-vah

This will stick you for a second

Esto va a picarle sólo por un segundo
es-to vah ah pee-car-leh so-lo por oon
seh-goon-do

The baby is very small and we are going to send it to the nursery for premature babies

La criatura es muy pequeña y vamos a
enviarla a el cuarto de crianza donde
tratan criaturas prematuras
la cree-ah-too-rah es moo-ee peh-keh-
nya ee vah-mos ah en-vyar-la ah el
coo-ar-to deh cryan-sa don-de trah-tan
cree-ah-too-ras preh-mah-too-ras

Do you want to breast feed your baby?

¿Quiere criar su criatura con el
pecho?
kye-reh cree-ar soo cree-ah-too-rah
con el peh-cho

You will go home in 5 days

Usted se irá a casa en cinco días
oos-teh seh ee-rah ah cah-sah en seen-
co dyas

98

CARDIOLOGY

CARDIOLOGIA
car-dyo-lo-hee-ah

Have you been under care for your heart?

¿Ha sido tratado (a) (fem.) del corazón?
ah see-do trah-tah-do (dah) del co-rah-son

Have you had high blood ?

¿Ha tenido presión alta de sangre?
ah teh-nee-do preh-syon al-tah deh san-greh

Have you had kidney diseases?

¿Ha tenido enfermedades de los riño-nes?
ah teh-nee-do en-fehr-meh-dah-des de los ree-nyo-nes

Scarlet fever?

¿Escarlatina?
es-car-lah-tee-nah

Rheumatic fever?

¿Fiebre reumática?
fee-eh-breh reh-oo-mah-tee-ca

Diphtheria?

¿Difterfa?
deef-teh-rya

Overweight?

¿Sobrepeso?
so-breh peh-so

Lues?

¿Sífilis?
see-fee-lees

Diabetes?

¿Diabetes?
dya-beh-tes

Arteriosclerosis?

¿Arterioesclerosis?
ar-teh-ryo-es-cleh-ro-sis

Liver diseases?

¿Enfermedades del hígado?
en-fehr-meh-dah-des del ee-gah-do

Do you have swollen ankles toward the end of the day?

¿Tiene los tobillos hinchados al final del día?
tye-neh los to-bee-lyos een-chah-dos al fee-nal del dya

Are the ankles of normal size when you get out of bed in the morning?

¿Están los tobillos de tamaño normal al levantarse por la mañana?
es-tan los to-bee-lyos de tah-mah-nyo nor-mal al leh-van-tar-seh por la mah-nya-nah

How many pillows do you use to sleep?

¿Cuántas almohadas usa para dormir?
kwan-tas al-mo-ah-das oo-sah pah-rah dor-meer

Do you wake-up nights with short-ness of breath and have to sit up to catch your breath?

¿Despierta durante las noches con la respiración corta y tiene que sentarse para respirar bien?
des-pyer-tah doo-ran-teh las no-ches con la res-pee-rah-syon cor-tah ee tye-neh keh sen-tar-seh pah-rah res-pee-rar

Are you short of breath on the slightest exertion?

¿Pierde la respiración al más pequeño esfuerzo?
pyer-deh la res-pee-rah-syon al mas peh-keh-nyo es-foo-er-so

Are you short of breath on climbing small hills, few steps or on walking?

¿Pierde la respiración subiendo pequeñas lomas, unos cuantos escalones, o caminando?
pyer-deh la res-pee-rah-syon soo-byen-do peh-keh-nyas lo-mas, oo-nos kwan-tos es-cah-lo-nes, o cah-mee-nan-do

Have you palpitations:

¿Tiene palpitaciones:
tye-neh pal-pee-tah-syo-nes

while resting?

mientras descansa?
myen-tras des-can-sah

while moving?

mientras se está moviendo?
myen-tras seh es-tah mo-vyen-do

Do you feel irregularities in your heart beats?

¿Siente usted irregularidades en sus palpitaciones del corazón?
syen-teh oos-teth ee-reh-goo-lah-ree-dah-des en soos pal-pee-tah-syo-nes del co-rah-son

Do you have pains accross the chest or pressure at times?

¿Tiene dolores sobre el pecho u opresión a veces?
tye-neh do-lo-res so-breh el peh-cho oo oh-preh-syon ah veh-ses

When?

¿Cuándo? kwan-do

... resting?

... descansando?
des-can-san-do

... moving?

... moviéndose?
mo-vyen-do-seh

... working?

                                      ... trabajando?
                                        trah-bah-han-do

... after a meal?

                                        ... después de comer?
                                        des-pwes deh co-mer

Are the pains agonizing with sense of impending death?

                                        ¿Son los dolores agonizantes con sensación de morir?
                                        son los do-lo-res ah-go-nee-san-tes con sen-sah-syon deh mo-reer

Do the pains radiate straight to the back and to the left arm?

                                        ¿Los dolores le van directamente a la espalda y al brazo izquierdo?
                                        los do-lo-res le van dee-rek-tah-men-teh ah la es-pal-dah ee al brah-so ees-kyer-do

How long the pains or the pressure or the tightness of the chest last?

                                        ¿Cuánto tiempo duran los dolores, o la presión, o la compresión del pecho?
                                        kwan-to tyem-po doo-ran los do-lo-res, o la preh-syon, o la com-preh-syon del peh-cho

What seems to relieve you?

                                        ¿Qué es lo que lo (a - fem.) alivia?
                                        keh es lo keh lo (ah - fem.) ah-lee-vya

How long have you been suffering?

                                        ¿Cuánto tiempo hace que usted sufre?
                                        kwan-to tyem-po ah-seh keh oos-teth soo-freh

Have you been taking medicines for the heart?

                                        ¿Ha estado tomando medicinas para su corazón?
                                        ah es-tah-do to-man-do meh-dee-see-nas pah-rah soo co-rah-son

                Which?

                                        ¿Cuáles?
                                        kwah-les

Have you spells of dizziness?

                                        ¿Tiene ataques de mareo?
                                        tye-neh ah-tah-kes deh mah-reh-o

... while walking?

                                        ... mientras camina?
                                        myen-tras cah-mee-nah

... while changing positions?

                                        ... mientras cambia de posición?
                                        myen-tras cam-bya deh po-see-syon

... while resting?

                                        ... mientras descansa?
                                        myen-tras des-can-sah

Do you fall when you get dizzy?	¿Se cae cuando se marea? seh cah-eh kwan-do seh mah-reh-ah
Do you become unconscious when you fall?	¿Queda inconsciente cuando se cae? keh-dah een-cons-syen-teh kwan-do seh cah-eh
Come into this room	Entre en este cuarto en-treh en es-teh kwar-to
Undress	Desvístase des-vees-tah-seh
Remove your:	Quítese su: kee-teh-seh soo:
coat	saco sah-co
blouse	blusa bloo-sah
vest	chaleco chah-leh-co
shirt	camisa cah-mee-sah
skirt	falda fal-dah
pants	pantalones pan-tah-lo-nes
petticoat	enaguas eh-nah-goo-as
brassiere	"brassiere" brahs-syer
shoes	zapatos zah-pah-tos
stockings	medias meh-dyas
socks	calcetines cal-seh-tee-nes
underwear	ropa interior ro-pah een-teh-ryor
panties	pantaloneta pan-tah-lo-neh-tah

Sit down

Siéntese
syen-teh-seh

Lie down

Acuéstese
ah-coo-es-teh-seh

Lie over your right side

Acuéstese sobre el lado derecho
ah-coo-es-teh-seh so-breh el lah-do
deh-reh-cho

Lie over your left side

Acuéstese sobre el lado izquierdo
ah-coo-es-teh-seh so-breh el lah-do
ees-kyer-do

Stand up

Póngase de pie
pon-gah-seh deh pyeh

Lift up your arm

Levante su brazo
leh-van-teh soo brah-so

Lift up your leg

Levante su pierna
leh-van-teh soo pyer-nah

Take these prescriptions

Tome estas recetas
to-meh es-tas reh-seh-tas

You need hospital care

Necesita cuidado de hospital
neh-seh-see-tah coo-ee-dah-do deh
os-pee-tal

Here is the note to enter the hospital

Aquí tiene la nota para entrar al
hospital.
ah-kee tye-neh la no-tah pah-rah entrar al os-pee-tal

Go home and stay in bed

Vaya a casa y permanezca en cama.
vah-yah ah cah-sah ee per-mah-nes-
cah en cah-mah

Stop working

Deje de trabajar.
deh-heh deh trah-bah-har

Return to work

Regrese a su trabajo
reh-greh-se ah soo trah-bah-ho

Call up your doctor to take care of
you

Llame su doctor para que se encargue
de usted.
lya-meh soo doc-tor pah-rah keh seh
en-car-gueh deh oos-teth

The reports of the tests will be sent to your doctor	Los informes de las pruebas serán enviados a su doctor. los een-for-mes deh las proo-eh-bas seh-rahn en-vya-dos ah soo doc-tor
You need x-rays of the chest	Usted necesita radiografías del pecho. oos-teh neh-ceh-see-tah rah-dyo-grah-fyas del peh-cho
You need an electrocardiogram	Usted necesita un electrocardiograma oos-teth neh-ceh-see-tah oon eh-lec-tro-car-dyo-grah-mah
You need blood chemistries and serology	Usted necesita pruebas químicas y serología de la sangre oos-teth neh-ceh-see-tah proo-eh-bas kee-mee-cas ee seh-ro-lo-hee-ah deh lah san-greh
Take a taxi home	Tome un taxímetro para ir a su casa to-meh oon tah-see-meh-tro pah-rah eer ah soo cah-sah
Walk slowly - do not climb stairs	Camine despacio - no suba escaleras. cah-mee-neh des-pah-syo - no soo-bah es-cah-leh-ras
Very glad to have served you	Muy contento en haberle servido moo-ee con-ten-to en ah-ber-leh ser-vee-do

ORTHOPEDICS

ORTOPEDIA
or-to-peh-dya

Were you born with this deformity?

¿Nació usted con este defecto?
nah-syo oos-teth con es-teh deh-fec-to

Did you have similar cases among
your ancestors?

¿Hubo casos similares entre sus
antecesores?
oo-bo cah-sos see-mee-lah-res en-treh
soos an-teh-seh-so-res

Does this deformity developed after
you were born?

¿Se le desarrolló este defecto después
de haber nacido?
seh leh deh-sah-rro-yo es-teh deh-
fec-to des-pwes deh ah-ber nah-see-do

Did you get any treatment or
operation for this condition?

¿Ha recibido algún tratamiento u operación por esta condición?
ah reh-see-bee-do al-goon trah-tah-
myen-to oo o-peh-ra-syon por es-tah
con-dee-syon

Does this defect followed an injury
or infection?

¿Le apareció el defecto después de un
accidente o infección?
leh ah-pah-reh-syo el deh-fec-to des-
pwes deh oon ac-see-den-teh o een-
fec-syon

What type of treatments were you
given?

¿Qué clase de tratamiento le han dado?
keh clah-seh deh trah-tah-myen-to leh
an dah-do

Did you meet with an accident?

¿Tuvo un accidente?
too-vo oon ac-see-den-teh

Explain how it happened

Explique cómo pasó.
eks-plee-keh co-mo pah-so

Where did it happen?

¿En donde le pasó?
en don-deh leh pah-so

While working?

¿Mientras trabajaba?
myen-tras trah-bah-hah-bah

In the street?

¿En la calle?
ehn lah cah-yeh

In your home?

¿En su casa?
ehn soo cah-sah

While riding a car, a train, a boat, or an airplane?

¿ Mientras viajaba en auto, en tren, en barco, o en aeroplano?
myen-tras vya-hah-bah en ah-oo-to, ehn trehn, en bar-co, o ehn ah-eh-ro-plah-no

When, and at what time the accident happened?

¿ Cuándo, y a qué hora pasó el accidente?
kwan-do, ee ah keh o-rah pah-so el ac-see-den-teh

Did you have a dizzy spell or faint before the accident?

¿ Se mareó o tuvo un desmayo antes del accidente?
seh mah-reh-o o too-vo oon des-mah-yo an-tes del ac-see-den-teh

Are you a compensation case?

¿ Es usted un caso de compensación?
es oos-teh oon cah-so deh com-pen-sah-syon

A liability case?

¿ Un caso de responsabilidad legal?
oon cah-so deh res-pon-sah-bee-lee-dad leh-gal

Are you insured?

¿ Está usted asegurado?
es-tah oos-teh ah-seh-goo-rah-do

What is the name and address of your insurer?

¿ Cuál es el nombre y la dirección de su asegurador?
kwal es el nom-breh ee lah dee-rec-syon deh soo ah-seh-goo-rah-dor

What is the name and adress of the place where you work?

¿ Cuál es el nombre y la dirección del sitio donde trabaja?
kwal es el nom-breh ee lah dee-rec-syon dehl see-tyo don-deh trah-bah-ha

Were you unconscious?

¿ Perdió el conocimiento?
per-dyo el co-no-see-myen-to

How long?

¿ Por cuanto tiempo?
por kwan-to tyem-po

What part of your body was hurt?

¿ Qué parte del cuerpo fué lastimada?
keh par-teh del kwer-po foo-eh las-tee-mah-dah

Were you taken to a hospital?

¿ Lo llevaron al hospital?
lo lyeh-vah-ron al os-pee-tal

Which?

¿ Cuál?
kwal

Did you have any bleeding form the nose, ears, or mouth?	¿Sangró por la nariz, orejas o boca? san-gro por la nah-rees, o-reh-has o bo-cah
Did you have water coming out from ears, nose or mouth?	¿Le salió agua por los oidos, nariz o la boca? leh sah-lyo ah-goo-ah por los o-ee-dos, nah-rees o la bo-cah
Did you lose control of any part of your body?	¿Perdió el control de alguna parte del cuerpo? per-dyo el con-trol de al-goo-nah par-teh del kwer-po
Do you have dizziness or headache?	¿Tiene vértigo o dolor de cabeza? tye-neh ver-tee-go o do-lor deh cah-beh-sah
Do you have nausea?	¿Tiene nausea? tye-neh nah-oo-seh-ah
Are you vomiting	¿Ha estado vomitando? ah es-tah-do vo-mee-tan-do
Are you short of breath?	¿Tiene falta de respiración? tye-neh fal-tah deh res-pee-rah-syon
When you breathe deeply, do you have sharp stabbing pains in the chest?	¿Cuando respira profundamente, tiene dolores punzantes dentro del pecho? kwan-do res-pee-rah pro-foon-dah-men-teh tye-neh do-lo-res poon-san-tes den-tro del peh-cho
Do you have pains in the abdomen?	¿Tiene dolores dentro del vientre? tye-neh do-lo-res den-tro del vyen-treh
Have you blood in the urine?	¿Tiene sangre en la orina? tye-neh san-greh en la o-ree-nah
Have you blood in the stool?	¿Tiene sangre en la excreta? tye-neh san-greh en la ex-creh-tah
Lift up your arms	Levante los brazos leh-van-teh los brah-sos
Lift up your legs	Levante sus piernas leh-van-teh soos pyer-nas
Make a fist	Haga un puño ah-gah oon poo-nyo

Extend your fingers	Enderese los dedos en-deh-reh-seh los deh-dos
Stand up	Póngase de pie pon-gah-seh deh pye
Bend over	Dóblese do-bleh-seh
Sit down	Siéntese syen-teh-seh
Bend backward	Dóblese para atrás do-bleh-seh pah-rah ah-tras
Lie down	Acuéstese ah-kwes-teh-seh
Flex your feet	Flexione los pies flek-syo-neh los pyes
Extend your feet	Extienda los pies ex-tyen-dah los pyes
Walk a few steps - back and forth	Camine unos cuantos pasos - para adelante y para atrás. cah-mee-neh oo-nos kwan-tos pah-sos pah-rah ah-deh-lan-teh ee pah-rah ah- tras
Are some of the fingers or toes numb?	¿Tiene alguno de los dedos de las manos o de los pies adormecidos? tye-neh al-goo-no de los deh-dos de las mah-nos o deh los pyes ah-dor-meh- see-dos
Have you tingling sensations?	¿Tiene hormigueo? tye-neh or-mee-geh-o
Can you open your mouth?	¿Puede abrir la boca? pwe-deh ah-breer la bo-cah
Can you chew?	¿Puede masticar? pwe-deh mas-tee-car
Do you see double?	¿Ve usted doble? veh oos-teh do-bleh
Bend your knees	Doble las rodillas do-bleh las ro-dee-lyas
Bend the elbows	Doble los codos do-bleh los co-dos

Rotate your hand

Vire la mano
vee-reh la mah-no

Rotate your ankle

Vire el tobillo
vee-reh el to-bee-lyo

Turn your head

Voltee la cabeza
vol-teh-eh la cah-beh-sah

   To the right

A la derecha
ah la deh-reh-cha

   To the left

A la izquierda
ah la ees-kyer-dah

Bend your head to the right

Doble la cabeza a la derecha
do-bleh la cah-beh-sah ah la deh-reh-
chah

Bend your head to the left

Doble la cabeza a la izquierda
do-bleh la cah-beh-sah ah la ees-kyer-
dah

Bend your head to the front

Doble la cabeza hacia el frente
do-bleh la cah-beh-sah ah-sya el fren-
teh

Bend your head to the back

Doble la cabeza hacia atrás
do-bleh la cah-beh-sah ah-sya ah-tras

You have:

Usted tiene:
oos-teth tye-neh

   A turn ligament or ligaments

Un o unos ligamentos rotos
oon o oo-nos lee-gah-men-tos ro-tos

   A fracture

Una fractura
oo-nah frac-too-rah

   A sprain

Una torcedura
oo-nah tor-seh-doo-rah

   A cyst

Un quiste
oon kees-teh

   A tumor

Un tumor
oon too-mor

   A cut nerve(s)

Un (o unos) nervio(s) cortado(s) (plural)
oon (o oo-nos) ner-vyos cor-tah-dos

   A cut blood vessel

Un (o unos) vaso (s) sanguineos cortado(s)
oon (o oo-nos) vah-so (s) san-gee-neh-o
(s) cor-tah-do(s)

You need to be operated

Necesita una operación
neh-seh-see-tah oo-nah o-peh-rah-syon

You need a cast

Necesita un entablillado
neh-seh-see-tah oon ehn-tah-blee-lya-
do

If the cast bothers you return
for recheck

Si el entablillado le molesta vuelva para
revisarlo
see el en-tah-blee-lya-do le mo-les-tah
voo-el-vah pah-rah reh-vee-sar-lo

If your toes, fingers or any part of
your extremities become swollen,
very red, dark, tingle, become numb
or very painful notify me at once

Si sus dedos o alguna parte de sus bra-
zos, piernas se hinchan, se vuelven rojas, se obscuresen, le dan hormigueo,
se le entumecen o le dan mucho dolor,
llámeme enseguida.
see soos deh-dos o al-goo-nah par-teh
de soos brah-sos pyer-nas seh een-chan
seh vwel-ven ro-has, seh obs-coo-reh-
sen, le dan or-mee-geh-o, seh le en-
too-meh-sen o le dan moo-cho do-lor,
lyah-meh-meh en-seh-gee-dah

Do not remove the cast, I will do it

No se quite el entablillado de yeso, yo
lo haré.
no seh kee-teh el en-tah-blee-lyah-do
de lye-so, lyo lo ah-reh

Keep your arm in a sling

Conserve su brazo suspendido con un
cabestrillo.
con-ser-veh soo brah-so soos-pen-dee-
do con oon cah-bes-tree-lyo

Stay in bed with a pillow under
the leg

Quédese en cama y ponga una almohada
debajo de la pierna.
keh-deh-seh en cah-mah ee pon-gah
oo-nah al-mo-ah-dah deh-bah-ho de la
pyer-nah

Put your hand (or foot) in warm water
for 30 minutes three times a day and
move the fingers

Ponga las manos (o los pies) en agua
caliente por 30 minutos 3 veces al día
y cierre y abra las manos.
pon-gah las mah-nos (o los pyes) en
ah-goo-ah cah-lyen-teh por trch-een-
tah mee-noo-tos tres veh-ses al dya ee
sye-rreh ee ah-brah las mah-nos

Exercise like this:
(Show the patient how)

Haga ejercicios de esta manera.
ah-gah eh-her-see-see-os deh es-tah
mah-neh-rah

Keep yourself resting for:	Descanse en casa por:
... days	... días dyas
... weeks	... semanas seh-mah-nas
... months	... meses meh-ses
You will need crutches	Va a necesitar muletas. vah ah neh-seh-see-tar moo-leh-tas
I am going to refer you to the Department of Physiotherapy	Voy a referirlo (a) (fem.) al departamen- to de fisioterapia para tratamiento. vo-ee ah reh-feh-reer-lo (ah) al deh-par- tah-men-to deh fee-syo-teh-rah-pya pah-rah trah-tah-myen-to
Take this note and go for treatment to ...	Tome esta nota y vaya para tratamiento al ... to-meh es-tah no-tah ee vah-lya pah-rah trah-tah-myen-to ahl ...
Apply an electric pad or hot water bag over the ...	Aplique un cojín eléctrico o bolsa de agua caliente sobre... ah-plee-keh oon co-heen eh-lec-tree-co o bol-sah deh ah-goo-ah cah-lyen-te so-breh ...
... times a day	... veces al día. ... veh-ses al dya
... minutes	... minutos. mee-noo-tos
Come back on:	Vuelva el: voo-el-vah ehl:
day	día .... dya
at ... a.m. or p.m.	a las ... de la mañana o de la tarde. ah las ... deh lah mah-nya-nah o deh lah tar-deh
year	año .... ah-nyo ...
Your are cured - and you are discharged	Usted está curado (a) (fem.) de alto(a) (fem.) oos-teth es-tah coo-rah-do (ah) ee leh do-ee deh al-to (ah)

Take this note and go for treatment
to ...

Apply an electric pad or hot water
bag over the ...

   ... times a day

   ... minutes

Come back on:

   day ....

   at ... a.m. or p.m.

   year ....

Your are cured - and you are
discharged

Descanse en casa por:

   ... días
   dyas

   ... semanas
   seh-mah-nas

   ... meses
   meh-ses

Va a necesitar muletas.
vah ah neh-seh-see-tar moo-leh-tas

Voy a referirlo (a) (fem.) al departamento de fisioterapia para tratamiento.
vo-ee ah reh-feh-reer-lo (ah) al deh-par-
tah-men-to deh fee-syo-teh-rah-pya
pah-rah trah-tah-myen-to

Tome esta nota y vaya para tratamiento
al ...
to-meh es-tah no-tah ee vah-lya pah-rah
trah-tah-myen-to ahl ...

Aplique un cojín eléctrico o bolsa de
agua caliente sobre...
ah-plee-keh oon co-heen eh-lec-tree-co
o bol-sah deh ah-goo-ah cah-lyen-te
so-breh ...

   ... veces al día.
   ... veh-ses al dya

   ... minutos.
   mee-noo-tos

Vuelva el:
voo-el-vah ehl:

   día ....
   dya

   a las ... de la mañana o de la tarde.
   ah las ... deh lah mah-nya-nah o deh lah
   tar-deh

   año ....
   ah-nyo ...

Usted está curado (a) (fem.) de alto(a)
(fem.)
oos-teth es-tah coo-rah-do (ah) ee leh
do-ee deh al-to (ah)

PEDIATRICS	PEDIATRÍA
	peh-dya-trya
Come in	Entre usted.
	en-treh oos-teh
When was the child born?	¿Cuándo nació la criatura?
	kwan-do nah-syo la crya-too-rah
Was the delivery normal?	¿Fué normal el parto?
	foo-eh nor-mal el par-to
Was an instrumental delivery?	¿Fué el parto llevado a cabo con el uso
	de instrumentos?
	foo-eh el par-to lyeh-vah-do ah cah-bo
	con el oo-so deh eens-troo-men-tos
Was a premature baby?	¿Fué la criatura prematura?
	foo-eh la cryah-too-rah preh-mah-too-
	rah
Is breast or bottle fed?	¿Alimenta la criatura con el pecho o
	la botella?
	ah-lee-men-tah la cryah-too-rah con el
	peh-cho o la bo-teh-lya
Did the baby have any illness after	¿Tuvo la criatura alguna enfermedad
delivery?	después de nacer?
	too-vo la crya-too-rah al-goo-nah en-
	fer-meh-dad des-pwes deh nah-ser
What formula do you give the child?	¿Qué fórmula le da a la criatura?
	keh for-moo-lah le dah ah lah crya-too-
	rah
Does the child eat well?	¿Come bien la criatura?
	ko-me byen la cree-ah-too-rah
Here you have a new formula	Aquí tiene una nueva fórmula.
	ah-kee tye-neh oo-nah nweh-vah for-
	moo-lah
How often you feed the child?	¿Qué tan amenudo alimenta la criatura?
	keh tan ah-meh-noo-do ah-lee-men-tah
	la cree-ah-too-rah
Moves the bowels and passes urine	¿Obra bien y pasa la orina normalmen-
normally?	te?
	o-brah byen ee pah-sah la o-ree-nah
	nor-mal-men-teh

Does the child sleep well?	¿Duerme bien la criatura? dwer-meh byen la cree-ah-too-rah
Does the child wet the bed?	¿Moja la cama la criatura? mo-ha la kah-mah la cree-ah-too-rah
Plays outdoors?	¿Juega al aire libre? hoo-eh-gah al ah-ee-reh lee-breh
How many hours?	¿Cuántas horas? kwan-tas o-ras
Takes vitamin?	¿Toma vitaminas? to-mah vee-tah-mee-nas
Has the child had:	Ha tenido la criatura: ah teh-nee-do la cree-ah-too-rah
Asthma?	¿Asma? ahs-mah
Chickenpox?	¿Viruelas locas? vee-rweh-las lo-kas
Diphtheria?	¿Difteria? deef-teh-rya
Mumps?	¿Paperas o parotidas? pah-peh-ras o pah-ro-tee-das
Scarlet fever?	¿Fiebre escarlatina? fee-eh-breh es-car-lah-tee-nah
Measles?	¿Sarampión? sah-ram-pyon
Pneumonia?	¿Pulmonía? pool-mo-nya
Cold?	¿Resfriados? res-fryah-dos
Rashes?	¿Erupciones? eh-roop-syo-nes
Has the child been vaccinated?	¿Ha sido vacunado? ah see-do vah-coo-nah-do
Any other injections?	¿Otras inyecciones? o-tras een-yek-syo-nes

Has the child had any operations or accidents?

¿Ha tenido la criatura alguna operación o accidente?
ah teh-nee-do la cree-ah-too-rah al-goo-nah o-peh-rah-syon o ak-see-den-teh

Has or had:

Tiene o ha tenido:
tye-neh o ah teh-nee-do

Fever?   How much?

¿Fiebre?   ¿Cuánta?
fyeh-breh   kwan-tah

Vomiting?   Of what?

¿Vómitos?   ¿De qué?
vo-mee-tos   deh keh

Coughing?   Day or night?

¿Tos?   ¿De día o de noche?
tos   deh dya o deh no-cheh

Convulsions?

¿Convulsiones?
con-vool-syo-nes

Spells of sneezing?

¿Ataques de estornudos?
ah-tah-kehs deh es-tor-noo-dos

Cries often?

¿Llora a menudo?
lyo-rah ah meh-noo-do

Is restles?

¿Es inquieto (a)?
es een-kyeh-to (ah)

Your next appointment is for .....
at .... p.m. or a.m.

Su próxima cita es para ... a las ...
p.m. o a.m.
soo prox-see-mah see-tah es pah-rah
... ah las .... peh ehm-meh o ah ehm-meh

Thanks for everything

Gracias por todo
grah-see-as por to-do

114

DENTISTRY	DENTISTERIA
	den-tees-teh-rya

Come in

Entre
en-treh

What is bothering you?

¿Qué le molesta?
keh le mo-les-tah

Sit in the chair

Siéntese en la silla.
syen-teh-seh en la see-lya

Open your mouth

Abra la boca
ah-brah la bo-cah

Where do you have pain?

¿Dónde tiene dolor?
don-deh tye-neh do-lor

Does it hurt more during the day or during the night?

¿Le duele mas durante el día o la noche?
leh dweh-le mas doo-ran-teh el dya o la no-cheh

What tooth hurts you?

¿Qué diente le duele?
keh dyen-teh le dweh-leh

Does it pain when you drink or eat hot things?

¿Le duele cuando bebe o come cosas calientes?
leh dweh-leh kwan-do beh-beh o co-meh co-sas cah-lyen-tes

Does it hurt on chewing?

¿Le duele al masticar?
leh dweh-leh al mas-tee-car

Does it hurt when you eat candy?

¿Le duele cuando come dulces?
leh dweh-leh kwan-do co-meh dool-ses

Do the gums bleed easily?

¿Le sangran las encías?
leh san-gran las en-syas

You have cavities

Usted tiene cavidades.
oos-teth tye-neh cah-vee-dah-des

You need fillings

Necesita empastaduras
neh-seh-see-tah em-pas-tah-doo-ras

I have to use the drill

Tengo que usar el taladro
ten-go keh oo-sar el tah-lah-dro

I have to pull out the tooth (or molar)

Tengo que sacar el diente (o muela)
ten-go keh sah-car el dyen-teh (o moo-eh-lah)

Dentistry

I am going to inject some medicine
to avoid pains

Voy a inyectarle medicina para evitar
dolor
voy ah een-yec-tar-leh meh-dee-see-
nah pah-rah eh-vee-tar do-lor

Bite the gauze for 20 minutes

Muerda la gasa por veinte minutos
moo-er-dah la gah-sah por veh-een-teh
mee-noo-tos

Rinse your mouth

Enjuágase la boca
en-hoo-ah-gah-seh la bo-kah

I am going to change the packing

Voy a cambiar el empaque
voy a kam-bee-ar el em-pah-keh

I am going to clean the teeth

Voy a limpiar los dientes
voy ah leem-pyar los dyen-tes

Eat only liquids and soft foods

Coma comidas blandas y tome líquidos
co-mah co-mee-das blan-das ee to-
meh lee¹kee-dos

Rinse your mouth with salt water
every .... hours - warm (or cold)

Enjuágase la boca con agua de sal cada
... horas - caliente (o fría)
en-hoo-ah-gah-seh la bo-cah con ah-
goo-ah deh sal cah-dah ... o-ras -
cah-lyen-teh (o frya)

Take the medicine every .... hours
or after meals
or before meals

Tome la medicina cada ... horas
después de las comidas
antes de las comidas
to-meh la meh-dee-see-nah cah-dah ...
o-ras des-pwes deh las co-mee-das
an-tes deh las co-mee-das

Do not remove the bridge until
you return

No se saque el puente antes de volver.
no seh sah-keh el pwen-teh an-tes de
vol-ver

Clean the bridge after each meal

Limpie el puente después de cada
comida
leem-pyeh el pwen-teh des-pwes deh
cah-dah co-mee-dah

Brush the teeth after each meal

Cepille los dientes después de cada
comida
seh-pee-lye los dyen-tes des-pwes deh
cah-dah co-mee-dah

The next visit will be on ...
at a.m. or p.m.

Su próxima visita será .... a las ....
a.m. o p.m.
soo prox-see-mah vee-see-tah seh-rah
... ah las ... ah ehm-meh o peh ehm-meh

If you cannot keep the appointment
cancel it - 24 hours in advance

Si no puede cumplir la cita - cancélela
veinte y cuatro horas antes.
see no pweh-deh coom-pleer la see-tah
   can-seh-leh-lah veh-een-teh ee
kwah-tro o-ras an-tes

It was a pleasure treating you -
good bye

Fué un placer tratarle - adios.
foo-eh oon plah-ser trah-tar-leh -
ah-dyos

LABORATORY	LABORATORIO lah-bo-rah-to-ree-o
How are you?	¿Cómo está usted? co-mo es-tah oos-teth
What do we have to examine?	¿Qué tenemos que examinar? ke teh-neh-mos ke ek-sah-mee-nar
The urine?	¿La orina? lah o-ree-nah
The blood?	¿La sangre? la san-greh
Blood count?	¿Cuenta de glóbulos? kwen-tah de glo-boo-los
The stool?	¿El excremento? el eks-creh-men-to
The sputum?	¿La esputa? la es-poo-tah
The vomitus?	¿El vómito? el vo-mee-to
Have you the doctor's written order?	¿Tiene la orden escrita del doctor? tye-neh la or-den es-cree-tah del dok-tor
Go to the bath room and put some urine in this container	Vaya al cuarto de baño y ponga orina en este recipiente vah-yah al kwar-to de bah-nyo ee ponga o-ree-na en es-teh reh-see-pyen-teh
Have you had breakfast?	¿Se ha desayunado usted? seh ah deh-sah-yoo-nah-tho oos-teth
Sit down	Siéntese syen-teh-seh
Make a fist	Haga un puño ah-ga oon poo-nyo
Open your hand	Abra su mano ah-bra soo mah-no
Bring back a stool specimen in this jar	Traiga una muestra de excremento en esta jarra trah-ee-ga oo-na moo-es-trah de ek-creh-men-to en es-ta hah-rrah

Bend your elbow

Doble su codo
do-bleh soo ko-do

Do not eat or drink after ....
o'clock

No coma o beba después de las ....
no co-mah o beh-bah des-pwes de las ...

Eat and return in:

Coma y vuelva en:
co-mah ee voo-el-vah ehn:

... minutes

... minutos
mee-noo-tos

... hours

... horas
o-ras

... days

... días
dyas

... weeks

... semanas
seh-mah-nas

... months

... meses
meh-ses

Your doctor will get the results
of the tests

Su doctor obtendrá los resultados de
las pruebas
soo dok-tor ob-ten-drah los reh-sool-
tah-thos de las proo-eh-bas

At your service, good bye

A sus órdenes, adios
a soos or-deh-nes, ah-dyos

SOCIAL SERVICE	SERVICIO SOCIAL ser-vee-syo so-see-al
Your name?	¿Su nombre? soo nom-bre
Your address?	¿Su dirección? soo dee-rek-syon
Your apartment number?	¿El número de su apartamiento? el noo-meh-ro de soo a-par-tah-myen-to
Your telephone number?	¿El número de su teléfono? el noo-meh-ro de soo teh-leh-fo-no
Your postal zone?	¿Su zona postal? soo so-nah pos-tal
How many rooms have you?	¿Cuántos cuartos tiene usted? kwan-tos kwar-tos tye-ne oos-teh
How many in your family?	¿Cuántos miembros en su familia? kwan-tos myen-bros en soo fah-mee-lya
Any other persons besides the family live with you?	¿Otras personas además de su familia viven con usted? o-tras per-so-nas a-deh-mas de soo fah-mee-lya vee-ven con oos-teth
How many adults?	¿Cuántos adultos? kwan-tos a-dool-tos
How many children?	¿Cuántos menores de edad? kwan-tos meh-no-res de eh-dad
How many beds?	¿Cuántas camas? kwan-tas cah-mas
Do you have a bathroom?	¿Tiene cuarto de baño? tye-ne kwar-to de bah-nyo
Do other families use the same bathroom?	¿Usan otras familias el mismo cuarto de baño? oo-san o-tras fah-mee-lyas el mees-mo kwar-to de bah-nyo
Do you have hot and cold water in your flat?	¿Tiene agua caliente y fría en el piso? tye-ne a-goo-ah cah-lyen-te ee frya en el pee-so

Is your apartment heated?	¿Tiene su apartamiento calefacción? tye-ne soo a-par-tah-myen-to cah-leh-fak-syon
Have you insects and rats and mice in your flat?	¿Hay insectos, ratas o ratones en su piso? ay een-sec-tos, ra-tas o ra-to-nes en soo pee-so
How many in the family are working?	¿Cuántos trabajan en la familia? kwan-tos trah-bah-han en la fah-mee-lya
How many of the children go to school?	¿Cuántos de los niños van a la escuela? kwan-tos de los nee-nyos van a la es-koo-eh-la
Do you belong to a society, club or parish?	¿Pertenece a alguna sociedad, club o parroquia? per-teh-neh-se a al-goo-na so-sye-dad cloob o pahr-ro-kee-ah
Have you, any society or parish helping your familia?	¿Tiene alguna sociedad o parroquia que lo ayudan? tye-ne al-goo-nah so-sye-dad o pah-ro-kee-ah ke lo a-yoo-dan
Who will take care of you when you leave the hospital	¿Quién lo cuidará cuando regrese del hospital? kyen lo koo-ee-dah-rah kwan-do re-gre-seh del os-pee-tal
Are you an American citizen?	¿Es usted ciudadano americano? es oos-teth see-oo-da-da-no a-meh-ree-kah-no
When did you come to the United States of America?	¿Cuándo vino a los Estados Unidos de América? kwan-do vee-no a los es-tah-dos oo-nee-dos de a-meh-ree-kah
How long have you lived in New York City?	¿Cuánto tiempo hace que vive en la ciudad de Nueva York? kwan-to tyem-po ah-se keh vee-veh en la see-oo-dad de noo-eh-va york

DIET AND NUTRITION	DIETA Y NUTRICION dye-tah ee noo-tree-syon
What is your age?	¿Cuál es su edad? kwal es soo e-dad
What is your weight?	¿Cuál es su peso? kwal es soo peh-so
What has been your maximum weight? When?	¿Cuál ha sido su peso máximo? ¿Cuándo? kwal ah see-do soo peh-so mak-see-mo kwan-do
What has been your minimum weight?	¿Cuál ha sido su peso mínimo? kwal ah see-do soo peh-so mee-nee-mo
What is your work?	¿Cuál es su trabajo? kwal es soo trah-bah-ho
How many hours do you work?	¿Cuántas horas trabaja? kwan-tas o-ras trah-bah-ha
At what time you get up?	¿A qué hora se levanta? ah keh o-ra se le-van-ta
At what time you go to bed?	¿A qué hora se acuesta? ah keh o-ra se a-kwes-ta
What do you eat in the morning, noon, and night?	¿Qué come en la mañana, mediodía, y en la noche? keh co-me en la mah-nya-na, meh-dyo-dya ee en la no-che
What do you eat between meals?	¿Qué come entre las comidas? keh co-me en-tre las co-mee-das
What do you eat before going to bed?	¿Qué come antes de acostarse? keh co-me an-tes de ah-cos-tar-se
Where do you eat your meals?	¿Dónde come sus comidas? don-de co-me soos co-mee-das
At home?	¿En su casa? en soo ca-sa
In a restaurant?	¿En el restaurante? en el res-tah-oo-ran-te
Carry them from home?	¿Se lleva las comidas de su casa? se yeh-vah las co-mee-das de soo ca-sa

How much coffee, tea or milk do you drink a day?	¿Cuánto café, té o leche toma al día? kwan-to ca-feh teh o leh-che to-ma al dya
Eat three times a day	Coma tres veces por día co-ma tres veh-ses por dya
What food or drinks upset your stomach?	¿Qué alimentos o bebidas le trastornan el estómago? keh ah-lee-men-tos o beh-bee-das le tras-tor-nan el es-to-mah-go
Do you drink alcoholic drinks - in moderation or excess?	¿Toma bebidas alcohólicas - en moderación o en exceso? to-mah beh-bee-das al-co-o-lee-kas - en mo-de-rah-syon o en ek-seh-so
Do not eat:	No coma: no co-ma
Greasy foods	Alimentos grasosos a-lee-men-tos gra-so-sos
Raw vegetables	Vegetales crudos veh-he-tah-les croo-dos
Pepper or spices	Pimienta ni otras especies pee-myen-ta nee o-tras es-pe-syes
Salt or baking soda	Sal o bicarbonato de soda sal o bee-car-bo-na-to de so-da
Sauces or gravies	Salsas sal-sas
Sugar or sweets	Azúcar o dulces a-soo-car o dool-ses
Use only unsalted butter	Use solamente mantequilla sin sal oo-se so-la-men-te man-teh-kee-ya seen sal
Do not drink alcoholic beverages	No tome bebidas alcohólicas no to-me beh-bee-das al-co-o-lee-kas

| X-RAY DEPARTMENT | DEPARTAMENTO DE RAYOS X |
| | de-par-tah-men-to de ra-yos eh-kees |

Good morning!
¡Buenos días!
bwe-nos dyas

Good afternoon!
¡Buenas tardes!
bwe-nas tar-des

Good evening!
¡Buenas noches!
bwe-nas no-ches

Sit down
Siéntese
syen-teh-se

What is your name and adress?
¿Cuál es su nombre y su dirección?
kwal es soo nom-breh ee soo dee-rek-syon

Your telephone number?
¿El número de su teléfono?
el noo-meh-ro de soo teh-leh-fo-no

Who is your doctor?
¿Quién es su doctor?
kyen es soo dok-tor

Do you have the written request from your doctor?
¿Tiene la orden escrita del doctor?
tye-ne la or-den es-cree-tah del dok-tor

What part of your body needs x-ray investigation?
¿Qué parte de su cuerpo necesita investigación?
keh par-te de soo kwer-po ne-seh-see-ta een-ves-tee-ga-syon

Are you a compensation case?
A liability case?
¿Es usted un caso de compensación?
¿O de corte?
es oos-teth oon ca-so de com-pen-sah-syon o de cor-te

Do you carry insurance?
¿Tiene usted algún seguro?
tye-ne oos-teth al-goon se-goo-ro

What is the name of the firm where you work?
¿Cuál es el nombre de la compañía donde trabaja?
kwal es el nom-bre de la com-pah-nya don-de trah-bah-ha

What is the address and telephone number of the company you work for?
¿Cuál es la dirección y el número de teléfono de la compañía donde trabaja?
kwal es la dee-rek-syon ee el noo-me-ro de te-le-fo-no de la com-pah-nya don-de trah-bah-ha

English	Spanish
Go into that room and remove your clothes	Vaya dentro de aquel cuarto y quítese la ropa vah-yah den-tro de a-kel kwar-to ee kee-teh-se la ro-pa
Put this gown on and wait until we call you	Póngase este camisón y espere hasta que le llamemos pon-gah-se es-te cah-mee-son ee es-pe-re as-ta keh le yah-meh-mos
Sit on this table	Siéntese sobre esta mesa syen-te-se so-bre es-ta meh-sa
Lay down:	Acuéstese: a-kwes-teh-se
Face down	Boca abajo bo-ca a-ba-ho
Face up	Boca arriba bo-ca a-ree-ba
Over right side	Sobre el lado derecho so-bre el la-do de-re-cho
Over left side	Sobre el lado izquierdo so-bre el la-do ees-kyer-do
Lift up:	Levante: le-van-te
The head	La cabeza la cah-beh-sa
The arm	El brazo el bra-so
The leg	La pierna la pyer-na
The buttocks	La asentadera la a-sen-tah-de-ra
Remain quiet	Esté muy quieto es-teh moo-ee kee-eh-to
Take a deep breath and hold it	Respire hondo y mantenga la respiración res-pee-re on-do ee man-ten-gah la res-pee-rah-syon

Breathe normally	Respire normalmente res-pee-re nor-mal-men-te
Breath out	Exhale ek-sah-leh
Breath in	Respire res-pee-reh
Stand perfectly still	Párese, completamente quieto pah-reh-se com-pleh-tah-men-te kye-to
Sit perfectly still	Siéntese completamente quieto syen-teh-se com-pleh-tah-men-te kye-to
Lie perfectly still	Acuéstese completamente quieto ah-kwes-te-seh com-pleh-tah-men-te kye-to
Get off from the table	Bájese de la mesa bah-he-seh de la meh-sa
Move over to the stretcher	Muévase sobre la camilla moo-eh-vah-se so-bre la cah-mee-ya
Sit on the wheel chair	Siéntese en la silla de ruedas syen-teh-seh en la see-ya de roo-eh-das
Return at	Vuelva a las ... voo-el-vah a las
Tomorrow	Mañana mah-nya-na
Morning	Por la mañana por la mah-nya-na
Afternoon	Por la tarde por la tar-de
This afternoon	Esta tarde es-ta tar-de
This evening	Esta noche es-ta no-che
Take this medicine tonight	Tome esta medicina esta noche to-me es-ta me-dee-see-na es-ta no-che

Do not take breakfast before the x-rays are taken	No tome desayuno antes de tomar los rayos x no to-me deh-sah-yoo-no an-tes de to-mar los rah-yos eh-kees
Take a laxative the night before you come here	Tome un purgante la noche antes de venir aquí to-me oon poor-gan-te la no-che an-tes de veh-neer ah-kee
Give yourself an enema before coming to have x-rays taken	Dese una enema (o lavativa) antes de venir a tomarse los rayos x. deh-se oo-na eh-neh-ma (o lah-vah-tee-vah) an-tes de veh-neer a to-mar-se los rah-yos eh-kees
Go to the bathroom and empty your bowels and pass the urine	Vaya al cuarto de baño y evacue y pase la orina vah-yah al kwar-to de bah-nyo ee eh-vah-kweh ee pah-se la o-ree-nah
I have finished taking all your x-rays	He terminado de tomar todos los rayos x eh ter-mee-nah-do de to-mar to-dos los rah-yos eh-kees
Get dressed	Vístase vees-tah-seh
I shall send the report to your doctor	Le enviaré el informe a su doctor leh en-vyah-reh el een-for-me ah soo dok-tor
It was a pleasure to do work for you	Fué un placer el hacer este trabajo para usted foo-eh oon plah-ser el ah-ser es-te trah-bah-ho pah-ra oos-teth

NURSING	ENFERMERÍA en-fer-meh-rya
Good morning!	¡Buenos días! bwe-nos dyas
Good afternoon!	¡Buenas tardes! bwe-nas tar-des
Good evening!	¡Buenas noches! bwe-nas no-ches
Have a good night	Tenga una buena noche ten-gah oo-na bwe-na no-che
Do you wish anything now?	¿Desea usted algo ahora? de-seh-a oos-teth al-go a-o-rah
Did you sleep well last night?	¿Durmió bien anoche? door-myo byen ah-no-che
Did you passed urine last night?	¿Orinó durante la noche? o-ree-no doo-ran-teh la no-che
How many times?	¿Cuántas veces? kwan-tas veh-ses
Did you move your bowels?	¿Ha obrado usted? ah o-brah-do oos-teth
Did you passed gas?	¿Ha pasado gas por el recto? ah pah-sah-do gas por el rek-to
Do you feel well or weak?	¿Se siente bien o débil? se syen-te byen o deh-beel
Do you want the door or window open or closed?	¿Quiere la puerta o la ventana abierta o cerrada? kye-re la poo-er-ta o la ven-tah-na ah-byer-tah o seh-rrah-da
Sit up	Siéntese syen-te-se
Out of bed	Fuera de la cama foo-e-ra de la cah-ma
Turn over your stomach	Voltee boca abajo vol-te-eh bo-ka a-ba-ho

Turn over right (left) side	Voltee sobre el lado derecho (izquierdo) vol-te-e so-bre el lah-do deh-re-cho (ees-kyer-do)
Turn over your back	Voltee boca arriba vol-te-e bo-ka a-ree-bah
You may go to the bath room	Puede ir al cuarto de baño pwe-de eer al kwar-to de bah-nyo
You do not go to the bath room	No puede ir al cuarto de baño no pwe-de eer al kwar-to de bah-nyo
I am going to take your temperature	Voy a tomarle su temperatura voy a to-mar-le soo tem-peh-rah-too-ra
Are you nauseated?	¿Está nauseado? es-ta nah-oo-se-a-tho
Are you dizzy?	¿Está mareado? es-ta mah-re-ah-do
Go to bed	Vaya a la cama va-ya a la cah-ma
You may get out of bed for a while today	Puede levantarse hoy por un rato pwe-de le-van-tar-se o-ee por oon ra-to
Drink a lot of water	Beba mucha agua be-ba moo-cha a-goo-a
Do you eat well?	¿Come bien? co-me byen
Do you like the meals	¿Le gustan las comidas? le goos-tan las co-mee-das
Shall I raise your head?	¿Quiere que le levante la cabeza? kye-re keh le le-van-te la cah-be-sa
Are you sleepy?	¿Tiene sueño? tye-ne soo-eh-nyo
Are you hot or cold?	¿Tiene calor o frío? tye-ne ca-lor o fryo
Ask for blankets if you need them	Pida mantas si las necesita pee-da man-tas see las ne-seh-see-ta

Do you want ventilation?	¿Quiere ventilación? kye-re ven-tee-la-syon
When you wish something, ring the bell	Cuando desee alguna cosa toque el timbre kwan-do de-se-e al-goo-na co-sa to-ke el teem-bre
I shall give you an enema	Le daré una enema le dah-re oo-na e-ne-ma
Do you have pains? Where?	¿Tiene dolores? ¿Dónde? tye-ne do-lo-res don-de
When is your family coming to see you?	¿Cuando viene su familia a verle? kwan-do vye-ne soo fah-mee-lya ah ver-le
I want to see them when they come in	Quiero verles cuando vengan kye-ro ver-les kwan-do ven-gan
I have finished	He terminado eh ter-mee-nah-tho

130

PHYSICAL EXAMINATION	EXAMEN FISICO ek-sah-men fee-see-ko
Disrobe completely	Desvístase del todo des-vees-tah-seh del to-do
Remove your:	Quítese su: (sus - soos - plural) kee-teh-se soo: (soos):
Coat	Saco sah-ko
Shirt	Camisa cah-mee-sah
Pants	Pantalones pan-tah-lo-nes
Socks	Calcetines kal-seh-tee-nes
Shoes	Zapatos sah-pah-tos
Blouse	Blusa bloo-sa
Petticoat	Refajo reh-fah-ho
Panties	Pantaloneta pan-tah-lo-ne-ta
Skirt	Falda fal-dah
Stockings	Medias meh-dyas
Brassiere	"Brassiere" brah-syer
Sit down	Siéntese syen-teh-se
Cross your legs	Cruce las piernas croo-seh las pyer-nas
Lay down	Acuéstese ah-kwes-teh-se

Lay down face down	Acuéstese boca abajo ah-kwes-teh-se bo-ka ah-ba-ho
Lay down face up	Acuéstese boca arriba ah-kwes-teh-se bo-ka ah-ree-ba
Lay down sideways	Acuéstese de lado ah-kwes-teh-se de la-do
Lay down over right side	Acuéstese del lado derecho ah-kwes-teh-se del la-do deh-reh-cho
Lay down over left side	Acuéstese del lado izquierdo ah-kwes-teh-se del la-do ees-kyer-do
Lift up your arm	Levante el brazo leh-van-te el bra-so
- the right	El derecho el deh-reh-cho
- the left	El izquierdo el ees-kyer-do
Lift up your leg	Levante su pierna leh-van-te soo pyer-na
Close your hand	Cierre la mano syeh-reh la mah-no
- tight	- apretada ah-preh-ta-tha
- lightly	- ligeramente lee-heh-rah-men-te
Bend your head forward	Doble la cabeza sobre el pecho do-bleh la cah-be-sa so-bre el peh-cho
Bend your head backward	Doble la cabeza hacia atrás do-bleh la cah-be-sa ah-sya ah-tras
Turn your head to the right	Voltee la cabeza a la derecha vol-teh-eh la cah-be-sa a la deh-reh-cha
Turn your head to the left	Voltee la cabeza a la izquierda vol-teh-eh la cah-be-sa a la ees-kyer-tha
Separte your knees	Separe sus rodillas seh-pah-reh soos ro-dee-yas

Cough	Tosa to-sah
Cough again	Tosa otra vez to-sah o-tra vez
Breathe	Respire res-pee-reh
Say thirty three every time I touch you	Diga treinta y tres cada vez que le toque dee-gah treh-een-tah ee tres ca-da vez keh le to-keh
Breathe in and out slowly with your mouth open	Respire para adentro y para afuera lentamente con la boca abierta res-pee-reh pah-rah ah-den-tro ee pah-rah ah-fwe-rah len-tah-men-teh con la bo-ca ah-byer-tah
Spread your legs wide apart	Abra las piernas lo más posible ah-brah las pyer-nas lo mas po-see-bleh
Press down as if you were going to move your bowels	Puje como si fuese a evacuar poo-he co-mo see foo-eh-seh ah eh-vah- kwar
Hold your breath	Detenga la respiración deh-ten-gah la res-pee-rah-syon
Point to the spot where you have the pain	Indíqueme la parte donde la duele een-dee-keh-meh la par-teh don-de le doo-eh-leh
Breathe rapidly with your mouth open	Respire rapidamente con la boca abierta res-pee-reh rah-pee-dah-men-teh con la bo-ca ah-byer-tah
Relax	Descanse usted des-can-seh oos-teth
Press down now	Puje ahora poo-he ah-o-rah
Do not be afraid	No se asuste no se ah-soos-teh
Please keep quiet	Sírvase tranquilizarse seer-vah-seh tran-kee-lee-sar-seh
Turn over on your side	Vuélvase sobre el lado voo-el-vah-seh so-bre el la-do

Turn over on your stomach	Vuélvase sobre el estómago voo-el-vah-seh so-bre el es-to-mah-go
Turn over on your back	Vuélvase sobre la espalda voo-el-vah-seh so-bre la es-pal-dah
This will not hurt you	Esto no le va a lastimar es-to no le vah ah las-tee-mar
This will hurt you but for a moment	Esto le molestará por un momento es-to le mo-les-tah-rah por oon mo- men-to
Does it hurt when I press here	¿Le duele cuando le aprieto aquí? le doo-eh-leh kwan-do le ah-prye-to ah-kee
Does the pain travel from this part to other parts?	¿Le corre el dolor de este punto a otras partes? le co-rreh el do-lor de es-teh poon-to ah o-tras par-tes
Is the pain worse when I press or when I let go suddenly?	¿Es el dolor peor cuando aprieto o cuando quito la mano de repente? es el do-lor peh-or kwan-do ah-prye-to o kwan-do kee-to la mah-no de reh- pen-teh
I am going to examine you by putting a finger in your rectum for a moment	Voy a examinarle a usted el recto con el dedo enguantado solo por un momento vo-ee ah ek-sah-mee-nar-le ah oos- teh el rek-to con el deh-do en-goo-an- tah-do so-lo por oon mo-men-to
Get up	Levántese leh-van-teh-seh
Get dressed	Vístese vees-teh-seh
Come back	Vuelva voo-el-vah
next week	la semana entrante la seh-mah-nah en-tran-teh
Monday	el lunes el loo-nes
Tuesday	el martes el mar-tes
Wednesday	el miércoles el myer-co-les

Come back next Friday	Vuelva el viernes voo-el-vah el vyer-nes
Come back next Saturday	Vuelva el sábado voo-el-vah el sah-bah-do
Come back next Sunday	Vuelva el domingo voo-el-vah el do-meen-go
Come in the	Venga en ven-gah en
morning	la mañana la mah-nyah-nah
afternoon	la tarde la tar-deh
night	la noche la no-cheh
At 1 o'clock	A la una ah la oo-nah
2 o'clock	A las dos ah las dos
3 o'clock	A las tres ah las tres
4 o'clock	A las cuatro ah las kwa-tro
5 o'clock	A las cinco ah las seen-ko
6 o'clock	A las seis ah las seh-ees
7 o'clock	A las siete ah las syeh-teh
8 o'clock	A las ocho ah las o-cho
9 o'clock	A las nueve ah las noo-eh-veh
10 o'clock	A las diez ah las dyes
11 o'clock	A las once ah las on-seh

At 12 o'clock	A las doce ah las do-seh
At 12 o'clock midnight	A las doce de la noche ah las do-seh de la no-cheh
At 12 o'clock noon	A las doce del mediodía ah las do-seh del meh-dee-o-dya
The halves and quarters of an hour	Las medias y cuartos de la hora: las meh-dyas ee kwar-tos de la o-rah
Come at 2:30 p.m.	Venga a las dos y media p.m. ven-gah ah las dos ee meh-dya peh eh- meh
Come at 2:30 a.m.	Venga a las dos y media a.m. ven-gah a las dos ee meh-dya ah eh-meh
The time of the day	La hora del día. la o-rah del dee-ah
Come at 2:30 in the morning	Venga a las dos y media de la mañana ven-gah ah las dos ee meh-dya de la mah-nyah-nah
Come at 2:30 in the afternoon	Venga a las dos y media de la tarde ven-gah ah las dos ee meh-dya de la tar-deh
Have you improved?	¿Ha mejorado usted? ah meh-ho-rah-do oos-teth
Come at 9:15 in the morning	Venga a las nueve y cuarto de la ma- nana ven-gah ah las noo-eh-veh ee kwar-to deh la mah-nyah-nah
Come at 3:45 in the afternoon	Venga a las tres y tres cuartos de la tarde ven-gah ah las tres ee tres kwar-tos deh la tar-deh
Come at 8:45 in the evening	Venga a las ocho y tres cuartos de la noche ven-gah ah las o-cho ee tres kwar-tos deh la no-cheh

TREATMENT INSTRUCTIONS	INSTRUCCIONES PARA TRATAMIENTOS
	eens-trook-syo-nes pah-rah trah-tah-myen-tos

I want you to use warm douches with vinegar

Quiero que usted use duchas de agua tibia con vinagre
kye-ro keh oos-teth oo-seh doo-chas de ah-goo-ah tee-bya con vee-nah-greh

Go home and stay in bed

Vaya usted a su casa y quédese en cama
vah-yah oos-teth ah soo cah-sah ee keh-deh-seh en cah-mah

I want you to take this medicine and come back here in one week

Quiero que tome esta medicina y vuelva dentro de una semana
kyeh-ro keh to-meh es-tah meh-dee-see-nah ee voo-el-vah den-tro de oo-na seh-mah-nah

Take one pill once a day

Tome una píldora una vez por día
to-meh oo-nah peel-do-rah oo-nah vez por dya

Take two tablets 2 times a day

Tome dos pastillas dos veces por día
to-meh dos pas-tee-yas dos veh-ses por dya

Take three capsules 3 times a day

Tome tres cápsulas tres veces al día
to-meh tres cap-soo-las tres veh-ses al dya

before meals

antes de las comidas
an-tes de las co-mee-das

after meals

después de las comidas
des-pwes de las co-mee-das

before going to bed

antes de acostarse
an-tes de ah-cos-tar-seh

when you wake up in the morning

cuando se levante por la mañana
kwan-do se leh-van-teh por la mah-nya-nah

Put a hot water bottle on the spot where it hurts you for half an hour, 5 times a day

Ponga una bolsa de agua caliente sobre la parte que le duele por media hora, cinco veces por día
pon-gah oo-nah bol-sah de ah-goo-ah cah-lyen-teh so-breh la par-teh keh le dweh-le por meh-dya o-rah, seen-co veh-ses por dya

You need an operation in order to
correct your condition, but don't
worry

Usted necesita una operación para
corregir su condición, pero no se
apure
oos-teth neh-seh-see-tah oo-nah o-peh-
rah-syon pah-rah co-rreh-heer soo
con-dee-syon, peh-ro no seh ah-poo-
reh

The nurse will make an appointment
for you

La enfermera le hará una cita
la en-fehr-meh-rah le ah-rah oo-nah
see-tah

Do not have sexual relations for
10 days

Es importante que no tenga relaciones
sexuales por diez días
es eem-por-tan-teh keh no ten-gah reh-
lah-syo-nes sek-soo-ah-les por dee-es
dyas

Take this medicine, one teaspoonful
alone, or with water, or milk, or
fruit juice, or soup

Tome esta medicina, una cucharadita,
sola, o con agua, o leche, o jugo de
fruta, o sopa
to-meh es-tah meh-dee-see-nah, oo-
nah coo-chah-rah-dee-tah, so-lah, o
con ah-goo-ah, o hoo-go de froo-tah,
o so-pah

Put two drops in two ounces of water

Ponga dos gotas en dos onzas de agua
pon-gah dos go-tas en dos on-sas de
ah-goo-ah

Put two drops into each:

Ponga dos gotas en cada:
pon-gah dos go-tas en cah-dah:

... nostril

... lado de la nariz
lah-do de la nah-reez

... eye

... ojo
o-ho

... ear

... oreja
o-reh-ha

Apply the ointment over:

Aplique el unguento sobre:
ah-plee-keh el oon-goo-en-to so-breh:

... the rash

... la erupción
la eh-roop-syon

... the wound

... la herida
lah eh-ree-dah

... the burn

... la quemadura
lah keh-mah-doo-rah

... the corn	... el callo el cah-lyo
... the painful area	... el área que le duele el ah-reh-ah keh le dweh-leh
Drink the medicine	Beba la medicina beh-bah la meh-dee-see-nah
Swallow the capsule, or the tablet, or the pill	Trague la cápsula, o la tableta, o la píldora trah-geh la cap-soo-lah, o la tah-bleh- tah, o la peel-do-rah
Apply a bandage and wet it every 2, 3 or 4 hours	Aplique un vendaje y mójelo cada 2, 3 o 4 horas ah-plee-keh oon ven-dah-he ee mo-heh lo cah-dah dos, tres o kwa-tro o-ras
Wet it with:	Mójelo con: mo-heh-lo con
... plain water	... agua sola ah-goo-ah so-lah
... saline solution	... agua de sal ah-goo-ah de sal
... Epsom salts solution	... Sulfato de magnesia sool-fah-to de mag-neh-sya
... this solution	... con esta solución con es-tah so-loo-syon
Put on an elastic bandage	Póngase un vendaje elástico pon-gah-seh oon ven-dah-heh eh-las- tee-ko
Take the medicine, one, two or three times a day	Tome la medicina, una, dos, o tres veces por día to-meh la meh-dee-see-nah, oo-nah, dos, o tres veh-ses por dya
Before, after, or between meals	Antes, después, o entre comidas an-tes, des-pwes, o en-treh co-mee- das
With water or without it	Con agua, o sin agua con ah-goo-ah, o seen ah-goo-ah
Swallow it. Do not swallow it	Tráguela, No la trague trah-geh-lah no la trah-geh

Do not chew it. Keep it in your mouth	No la mastique. Déjela en la boca. no la mas-tee-keh deh-heh-lah en la bo-kah
You can take it with:	Puede tomarla con: pwe-deh to-mar-lah con:
fruit juice	jugo de fruta hoo-go de froo-tah
milk	leche leh-che
coffee	café cah-feh
tea	té teh
soup	sopa so-pah
Let it melt on your tongue	Deje que se derrita sobre su lengua deh-he keh seh deh-ree-tah so-breh soo len-goo-ah
Take it:	Tómela: to-meh-lah
In the morning	Por la mañana por la mah-nyah-nah
In the afternoon	Por la tarde por la tar-deh
In the evening	Por la noche por lah no-cheh
At bedtime	Al acostarse al ah-cos-tar-seh
During the night	Durante la noche doo-ran-teh la no-cheh
Take a teaspoonful	Tome una cucharadita to-meh oo-nah coo-chah-rah-dee-tah
Take a tablespoonful	Tome una cucharada to-meh oo-nah coo-chah-rah-da
Take one pill	Tome una píldora to-meh oo-nah peel-do-rah

Take a lozenge

Tome una oblea
to-meh oo-nah o-bleh-ah

Take a tablet

Tome una tableta
to-mch oo-nah tah-bleh-tah

Take a capsule

Tome una cápsula
to-meh oo-nah cap-soo-lah

Take it:

Tómela:
to-meh-lah

Every hour

Cada hora
kah-dah o-rah

Every two hours

Cada dos horas
kah-dah dos o-ras

Every three hours

Cada tres horas
kah-dah tres o-ras

Every four hours

Cada cuatro horas
kah-dah kwa-tro o-ras

Every five hours

Cada cinco horas
kah-dah seen-ko o-ras

Every six hours

Cada seis horas
kah-dah seys o-ras

Chew the medicine before
swallowing it

Mastique la medicina antes de tragarla
mas-tee-keh la meh-dee-see-nah an-tes de trah-gar-lah

Take the medicine only if you
have pains

Tome la medicina solamente en caso de dolor
to-meh la meh-dee-see-nah so-lah-men-teh en kah-so de do-lor

Put your foot, or hand, or leg or
arm in hot water

Ponga el pie, la mano, la pierna, el brazo en agua caliente
pon-gah el pye, la mah-no, la pyer-nah el brah-so en ah-goo-ah kah-lyen-teh

For five, ten, fifteen, twenty, thirty,
forty, fifty, or sixty minutes

Por cinco, diez, quince, veinte, treinta, cuarenta, cincuenta o sesenta minutos
por seen-ko, dyez, keen-seh, veyn-te treh-een-tah, kwa-ren-tah, seen-kwen-tah o seh-sen-tah mee-noo-tos

Take a sitz bath

Tome un baño de asiento
to-meh oon bah-nyo de ah-syen-to

With hot water	Con agua caliente con ah-goo-ah kah-lyen-teh
With cold water	Con agua fría con ah-goo-ah frya
Change the bandage every ...	Cambie el vendaje cada ... kam-bye el ven-dah-heh cah-da
Keep your bandage wet	Conserve el vendaje mojado con-ser-veh el ven-dah-he mo-hah-do
Wet it every ... hours	Mójelo cada ... horas mo-heh-lo cah-da ... o-ras
Dissolve a tablespoonful of kitchen salt in a quart of water	Disuelva una cucharada de sal de co- cina en un litro de agua dee-soo-el-vah oo-nah coo-chah-rah- da de sal de co-see-nah en oon lee-tro de ah-goo-ah
Use hot (or cold) compresses every ... hours	Use compresas calientes (o frías) cada ... horas oo-seh com-preh-sas kah-lyen-tes (o fryas) cah-dah ... o-ras
Return in:	Vuelva en: voo-el-vah en:
... days	... días dyas
... weeks	... semanas seh-mah-nas
... months	... meses meh-ses
... years	... años ah-nyos

NOTES

NOTES

NOTES